"*Work-life balance sounds great on paper. In practice it's about promises made to those we value most, and ourselves, too. How easy it is not to fulfil those promises. Nadim Saad's book offers sensible and practical solutions for working parents, and some great tips for bringing up happy, balanced kids.*"

John Lees – Author of How to Get a Job You Love

"*With more children than ever being brought up in households where both parents work, there is a real need for practical resources that help working parents enjoy stress-free time with their kids. The Working Parents Guide is clearly-laid-out and it is full of tips and tools that will help parents balance work and family time successfully.*"

**Tanith Carey – Author of Mum Hacks,
Taming the Tiger Parent and Girls, Uninterrupted**

"*The Working Parents' Guide is an invaluable resource for working parents who want to improve their work-life balance and have a more enjoyable family life. The parallels between leadership and parenting made in the book are inspiring and bring great awareness of our role as parents and leaders. I also really enjoyed the leadership quotes that illustrate each technique in the book. I highly recommend it.*"

**Jérôme Ballarin – Founder and Chairman of the
Observatory of Work-Life balance and Parenthood in Business**

"*Nadim Saad has created a well structured, user friendly and most importantly, effective manual that gets to the heart of the issues that impact real families. Bite-sized chapters and an accessible style of writing will enable parents to dip in and out according to the particular needs of their situation and without feeling preached to (something no parent wants). This is a book that will certainly be informing my own work with families.*"

Gary Leboff – Performance Psychologist and Author of Dare

THE WORKING PARENTS' GUIDE

to raising
happy and confident
children

Kids Don't Come With a Manual
Series

NADIM SAAD

First published in the United Kingdom by
Best of Parenting Publishing
242 Acklam Road, London, W10 5JJ, United Kingdom
www.bestofparenting.com

ISBN: 978-0-9931743-7-7

Editor Jacq Burns, www.jacqburns.com

Cover Design and typesetting by Danijela Mijailović

Set in Minion Pro

Printed and bound in Great Britain by Clays Ltd., St Ives plc

To the love of my life Carole, thank you for leading
the way and showing me I can become a better parent,
and for helping me discover my passion for parenting.
Thank you also for your dedication in raising our children.

To my parents, thank you for all your love,
dedication and support all these years.

To my daughters Noor, Yasmine and Yara,
thank you for helping me grow and become
a better human being and parent.
You are the light, the magic and the joy of my life.

To Elizabeth,

I hope this will prove useful
and I look forward to
our potential collaboration

Nadim

Contents

Introduction

The struggle of working parents

When our kids are born, we are faced with a plethora of new responsibilities. It's quite amazing that we manage to fit in so many additional child-raising activities to already full lives.

As working parents, we are more likely to feel under pressure to make the time that we get to spend with our children 'count'. We are also prone to feeling guilty when we don't spend as much time with them as we would like. Struggling with work-family balance is one of the most stressful aspects to parenting and this book's aim is to help.

The reality is that parenthood comes with all sorts of challenges. Through our experience of running parenting courses and workshops with thousands of working parents and the hundreds of thousands of queries on our Best of Parenting app, we found that most parents invariably share the same struggles of:

- Trying to get kids out of the house in the morning on time - or going to bed - without having to resort to shouting, threatening or rewarding

- Experiencing a general lack of cooperation from children and dealing with their amazing capacity to ignore what we're telling them

- Trying to cope with kids whining, complaining and having tantrums

- Having arguments over food, homework and many other things

- Our children being rude, including back-chatting and arguing

- Managing sibling rivalry and children competing for parental attention

These challenges can be accentuated by the pressures that work places on the time we spend with our children. When we look for advice, there are thousands of parenting experts who spell out conflicting theories about parenting – so who do we listen to? It is no wonder that many parents find themselves being uncertain as to how to parent. And so the approach parents take may end up depending on our mood, stress levels, and the 'association' that each situation holds for us.

Many of us arrive home from work, feeling tired and wanting to put our feet up only to feel guilty for not spending as much time with our kids as we would like to. We may therefore overcompensate by becoming more lenient and/or rewarding our children with gifts or treats. Conversely, some working parents may think 'I have such little time with my children that I have to make sure I set them boundaries and instil values'. In this case, we are likely to spend more time disciplining our children, and the time pressure is likely to increase our stress levels. This in turn will make the time we do get to spend with our children less enjoyable.

The stressors of family life are therefore likely to affect our work and vice versa, as the stress of work can also easily spill into our life at home. So although we may try to separate our work from our family life - usually for very valid reasons - the reality is that the two are much more interlinked than we might think.

Work-family harmony

In fact, leading thinkers now explain that the concept of work-life balance is misleading because it is based on the idea that 'work' competes with 'life'. Wharton professor, Steward Friedman, an expert on the matter, prefers to talk about the importance of achieving better 'work-life harmony' or 'work-life integration'. He argues that our goal should be to create harmony between work and life instead of thinking only in terms of trade-offs[1].

Unfortunately, this change of appellation doesn't make work-life harmony any easier to achieve! However, it is useful in the sense that it helps us to realise that rather than trying to separate work and family life, we might be able to better manage our lives by acknowledging the links between them. And that's where I realised the need for this book. I had thoroughly researched the best of parenting practice, and saw that there was a lot in common between the best practice of good parenting and the best practice of good leadership.

One of the broad definitions of leadership is that it is the process of using our social influence to guide people towards the achievement of specific goals or outcomes[2]. And as former US President D.D. Eisenhower defined it: "Leadership is the art of getting someone else to do something you want done because he wants to do it". Isn't this exactly what we are trying to achieve with our children every day?

One of the other common traits between parenting and leadership is that both are skills that can be developed. As with all other aptitudes that we use in the workplace, it requires some knowledge, training and practice. However, there are good reasons why as parents, we often fall short of developing our parenting skills:

- We don't usually get any training - other than pre-natal classes for some and rarely some parenting classes.

- Although we tend to glean knowledge left and right from family, friends or on the internet, the advice we get is often conflicting and seldom based on research, even when it comes from parenting books.

- In terms of practice, we get lots of it, but we don't actually see the effect of what we do until much later in life when our kids are older, by which time it is more difficult to make up for our potential mistakes.

Putting parenting and leadership together

Like many working parents I've interviewed in my coaching practice, I used to think: 'When I come home from work, I just want to relax, unwind and be myself'.

I had created and expanded companies of different sizes in three continents and with very diverse teams. In the process, I drew on the many managerial and leadership skills that I learnt during my MBA and from leadership workshops. However, when I became a parent, I didn't consciously think about using these skills at home.

What changed my thinking was that while coaching parents, a great many of whom also happened to be managers and leaders, I encountered several situations that made me realise that there are strong parallels between leadership and parenting. In recognising these parallels, it became clear to me that the skills that we develop in the workplace can be much more useful at home than I had first expected:

1. A significant number of working parents who've attended our Best of Parenting courses noted that many of the skills and techniques that we were teaching them to use at home were skills that they were already familiar with using in the workplace. And those who weren't already using them started to use some of these tools, not only in their family lives but also at work, and found that they were as effective in the workplace as they were at home.

2. Before I learnt a lot of these new techniques, I was a Strict/Authoritarian Dad (see Tool #1 - **Understanding Your Strengths and Weaknesses**). I would often let my emotions take over so I would end up shouting and getting angry at home, while I had a much more agreeable style with my colleagues - as I had better 'boundaries' at work. My wife kept asking me to treat her and the kids more like I was treating my staff and colleagues at work.

My answer was invariably that my work and my family life were unrelated and that she couldn't expect me to treat her like my colleagues, while she was also expecting me to be much more caring and 'emotionally involved' at home. The reality is that despite not wanting to admit it openly, I did realise that it's also important to have healthy boundaries at home and respect my loved ones, as they are the people who are closest to me and on whom my behaviour has the strongest impact.

However, I needed hard facts and research to convince me to change. A defining moment for me was when I learnt that a lot of the things that I was doing 'for my children's own good', such as lecturing them and shouting at them, were actually making it harder for them to comply. Moreover, I discovered that the conclusions of the latest research in neuroscience and child rearing have a lot in common with the best practice in leadership. This meant that many of the common sense techniques that we use in the workplace to better lead teams are the same that we should be using at home. The challenge that remained was to put these common sense techniques into 'common practice' and this is what I set out to achieve.

This new awareness led to my wife, Carole - an experienced teacher turned parenting coach - and I setting up Best of Parenting. We used our experience and did extensive research to develop a set of step-by-step tools that blend existing tried and tested parenting methods with the latest research in child psychology, behaviour and neuroscience. When we used our tools on our own family, the effect was genuinely life changing.

We ended up writing a highly acclaimed parenting book entitled *Kids Don't Come With a Manual – The Essential Guide to a Happy Family Life*. It was intended as a reference book and is very comprehensive as a result; it is in essence a 'best of' all the research and methods that we discovered in our years of research. Yet, I felt deep inside that I should write a book that was adapted specifically for working parents. I knew that, if I used to be put off by long parenting books because I didn't have the time and didn't find them practical enough, then there was a strong chance that there were lots of other working parents out there who felt the exact same way.

I was already teaching best parenting practices to working parents within leading organisations by invoking and using best leadership practices. So I set out to write a book that would bring together these best practices and that would make perfect sense to working parents and help to simplify life all round.

This Book's Objective

I realised that all busy working parents could benefit from a shorter book full of hard facts and practical tips, that they can dip in and out of as they see fit. I also thought that working parents could better understand and assimilate the best practice of child rearing if they realised that the 'soft skills' that we are trained to use in the workplace can prove to be just as effective in resolving typical parenting challenges.

The Working Parents' Guide therefore contains a series of tools and techniques that are designed to help you - busy working parents - to:

1. Resolve typical parenting challenges effectively in the short-term and limit the recurrence of misbehaviour.

2. Always focus on the longer-term goal of raising your children to become happy, confident and resilient adults.

As you read this book, you will realise that you already have a lot - if not all - of the skills that you need to be able to deal with most challenges that inevitably accompany family life. This book is here to provide the missing link and help you utilise these skills to full effect at home.

My intention is not to make working parents feel like they are being 'measured' (as we already go through enough appraisals at work!), nor is it about making family life run more like a business. For most working parents, it's essential that when we walk through the door after a busy day at work, we are able to draw a line between our professional selves and our personal selves. Typically, we don't want to think of ourselves as a manager when we are at home, we just want to be ourselves and be able to enjoy spending time with our children.

This book isn't here to change that - it's not about implementing rigid business processes at home or trying to become the perfect parent. Too many parents are already made to feel like failures by media and literature that pressurises us to live up to an idealised notion of 'parenting perfection' at all times.

This book will hopefully provide an antidote to this, as its intention is to provide you with a toolkit so that you have the choice to react more effectively when faced with typical parenting challenges. It will also enable you to better define what works best for you and for your child, and make your home life happier and easier.

However, leadership is not easy - not in the workplace or in our homes. It's not as straightforward as 'management' (see **Chapter 1**), and it's far more time-consuming. It involves coaching, modelling, patience, do-overs, problem-solving, listening, teaching and being very thoughtful in our communication. As time-consuming as it is, becoming a Leader parent (more on this in **Chapter 2**) is *worth it* - knowing our kids will learn to respond from a place of trust rather than responding out of fear-based obedience.

The aim is to make you feel that while you may not always be perfect and are bound to make mistakes and lose it at times, you always have a choice to keep the connection with your children strong and maximise their chances of becoming happy and confident.

How to get the most out of this book

We appreciate that every child is different and as their parent, you are the one who knows them best, so this book is designed for you to use it in the way that best works for you.

Each of the 7 chapters - apart from chapter 1 - contains a series of tools (22 in total). Each tool can be read independently of the rest so it's easy to dip in and out of the book at any time. You can choose to use the tools that are most relevant to your children's characters and needs at different times and depending on their age.

Each tool explains how the best practice in leadership and child rearing can be applied at home with practical examples of application. It also contains a scenario that is based on real-life examples, taken from our experiences with our children and the thousands of parents that we have coached.

Each chapter ends with a summary, which highlights the key points of each section so that you have a quick and easy way to reference the book's central ideas without having to reread the whole chapter. There are also pages at the end of each chapter for you to make notes, brainstorm ideas or record your progress.

The book also contains bonus material which is key to getting the most out of this book:

1. A 5-Week Programme, which suggests a handful of tools to read each week and that requires only 10 minutes per day. This series of tools will enable you to achieve specific goals each week (such as improving cooperation or making your children more responsible). The programme also provides a useful timeframe so that you know when you can expect to start seeing results. The key to following this programme is that consistency and a certain amount of accountability are essential in implementing change. So if you are committed to improving your relationship with your children, this programme will be of great help.

   This programme ends with some suggestions of tools that you can share with secondary carers such as relatives, child minders or nannies so that they can better understand your approach and how you would like your kids to be taken care of.

2. A troubleshooting section with suggestions on how to use the tools in this book to resolve 20 of the most common parenting challenges, including tantrums, morning and bedtime issues, homework and sibling squabbles. If you find yourself faced with a pressing parenting issue that you need to resolve, you can jump straight to this troubleshooting section as this provides references to the tools - and examples of how to use them - that are specifically designed to help you overcome your specific challenge.

Of course, you can read the book all at once - this will provide you with a more comprehensive understanding of all the tools and techniques and a general 'framework' that you can use to improve your parenting skills and transform your family life. However, it is usually more effective not to implement too many tools at once, as children usually don't react too well to extreme changes in their parents' behaviour. Implementing just a few tools at a time will also enable you to understand which tools are working best with your child, and this is where the 5-Week Programme can help.

Finally, if you'd like to discover more about our personal experiences as parents and discover stories and anecdotes from other parents, you can visit our website www.bestofparenting.com and register to our free newsletter or our online video course.

CHAPTER 1

What Parenting and Leadership have in common

"Before you are a leader, success is all about growing yourself.
When you become a leader, success is all about growing others."
Jack Welch, Former CEO of General Electric,
Author of *Winning*

Once we become a parent, we develop several skills that can be very useful in the workplace. We should be aware of and honour these skills. Here is a brief overview of some of the ways in which the skills we acquire as parents can help to strengthen our effectiveness in the workplace:

Being flexible: When we have children, we have to learn to 'go with the flow', and not allow ourselves to get frustrated on the occasions when we have to change our plans at the last minute. This skill is particularly useful, because when you're a parent, plans tend to change quite often! This can be difficult for more controlling personalities, but if we learn to be more flexible in all areas of our lives then this can also have a positive impact upon our performance at work.

Multitasking: We usually become a champion multitasker. Have you ever held your phone with one hand while changing a nappy and giving your child milk at the same time? Learning to juggle multiple priorities simultaneously can make us sharper and more decisive, which are essential skills in the corporate world.

Prioritising: As a result of having to juggle several things at once, we also end up becoming more aware of the importance of prioritising. We learn to prioritise usually to ensure that we can e office on time to pick up our children, or so that we

room in our schedule to spend more time with them.

olling emotions: This doesn't always come naturally and we might go through a phase of feeling like we have even less control over our emotions than we did before we became parents. Parenthood brings all sorts of strong feelings to the surface, which are not always rational as they are often related to our childhood experiences. But with practice, most of us learn to better regulate our emotions both at home and in the workplace - this book will give you plenty of ideas of how to improve your ability to control your emotions.

Empathy and compassion: Having kids helps us to put ourselves in other people's shoes and can make us more compassionate with our colleagues at work.

Maturity and understanding of ourselves: Having children means that we will often need to 'parent our inner child'. This allows us to have a better understanding of what shaped us into becoming an adult, as well as our most important values and what really matters to us.

Leadership and Parenting have a lot in common

Most people think of leaders as belonging to the corporate world and don't associate being a leader with being a parent. However, when we look at what it means to be a leader in its broadest sense, it becomes apparent that parenting and leadership are very closely linked. The primary thing that they have in common is that both parents and leaders work towards a specific outcome through the leadership of people. Let's look at some of the other key things they have in common:

1. There are different styles and approaches when it comes to leadership. Some managers tend to micro-manage their staff while others are a lot more 'hands-off'; some managers have more of a top-down approach while others tend to be more collaborative. There is no right or wrong way to lead people and leadership involves a lot of learning 'on the job' with trial and error to find the

most effective leadership style. However, extensive research on leadership demonstrates that there are certain leadership approaches that are more effective than others.

This is equally true of parenting. There are different parenting styles and there is no right or wrong way to parent, as a lot of our experience is based on understanding the individuality of our children and will therefore involve trial and error. However, there is now a wealth of research that demonstrates that certain approaches and techniques are far more effective than others, and we will explore these over the course of this book.

2. The most effective leaders have a vision and strategy in mind for what they want their team to achieve or become and take active steps to ensure their vision is realised.

The most effective parents have a vision and strategy in mind for what they want their children to become (kind, happy, independent, successful, etc.) and will do everything they can to maximise the chances of this happening.

3. Leaders may have some character traits in common, but *"Leaders aren't born, they are made. And they are made just like anything else, through hard work."* - **Vince Lombardi**. The best leaders are therefore the ones who focus on practicing and honing their leadership skills.

Similarly, there are no personality traits that guarantee we will make a great parent; the best parents are the ones who recognise that their skills and abilities as parents need to be honed and developed, and this comes with practice, patience and dedication.

4. As renowned INSEAD professor Herminia Ibarra's research and latest book 'Act Like a Leader, Think Like a Leader' explain, not only can leadership be taught, but the best way to become a leader is to start acting like a leader. Acting like a leader is far more effective than just thinking about the type of leader we want to become. Change happens as a result of action rather than thoughts and words alone, as changing our actions and behaviour has the

effect of also changing our mindset. So acting like a leader creates a self-reinforcing cycle that helps improve our existing skills and increases the chances of one day actually becoming a leader. Dr. Ibarra calls this concept 'Outsight'.

This is equally true of parenting. Our parenting style isn't something that can easily be changed, which means that it can be very difficult to think ourselves into becoming a better parent as most of us are typically ingrained in our 'learnt' thought patterns. However, jumping into having new experiences and approaching everyday situations in a different way sets us free from the limitations of old habits and unhelpful thought patterns. It changes our perspective so that we are able to redefine what we are capable of. In other words, when we start applying new parenting techniques, sooner or later they will become second nature. This is why this book is full of techniques taken from the best practice in leadership and parenting to make them actionable and create 'Outsight'. In doing this, we create a self-reinforcing cycle that enables us to become a better parent once we apply them consistently.

5. Leadership entails using our social influence to guide people towards the achievement of specific goals or outcomes. As the quotes below illustrate so well, the basis of effective leadership is to use our influence, understanding and trust, rather than our power or authority, to guide our team towards a shared goal or outcome. And this is what differentiates true 'leadership' from just 'management':

- *"Management is about arranging and telling. Leadership is about nurturing and enhancing"* – **Tom Peters, Best Selling Author of In Search of Excellence**

- *"There is a difference between being a leader and being a boss. Both are based on authority. A boss demands blind obedience; a leader earns his authority through understanding and trust."* **Klaus Balkenhol, Olympic Champion**

- *"The key to successful leadership is influence, not authority."* **Kenneth H. Blanchard, Best Selling Author of the One Minute Manager**

Similarly, the most effective parents use their *influence*, rather than their power or authority, to guide their children towards fulfilling their potential and maximise their chances of thriving in adult life. As Thomas Gordon, author of Parent Effectiveness Training explains: *"You acquire more influence with young people when you give up using your power to control them … as the more you use your power to try to control people, the less influence you'll have on their lives."* [3]

Despite these interesting commonalities, there are obviously also fundamental differences between being a leader in the workplace and being a leader at home:

1. We cannot reason with children in the same way that we can reason with an adult. We will see in **Chapter 2** that a child's pre-frontal cortex, which is responsible for most of their reasoning, is in development until the age of 25 (see Tool # 3 - **Understanding Your Children**). This means that children cannot understand the consequences of their actions as well as an adult, and the challenge is therefore to adapt our communication to their level of understanding.

2. There are usually a lot more emotions involved in parenting. Our children are more likely to bring out emotions that are related to our own childhood and 'push our buttons', which often makes it harder to react rationally at home. It is important to identify these 'triggers' and replace them with more effective alternatives and some of the tools are devised to do exactly this.

3. We cannot fire our kids whatever mistakes they make! We therefore do not have this ultimate threat at our disposal and as their guardians, we are ultimately responsible for their actions. We therefore have to find more effective ways to get them to do what they are supposed to do without unnecessary threats. We also need to help them become active and responsible members of their community and wider society by the time they leave our home.

4. Parenting can also deviate from the corporate world, as salaries are often the key driver in motivating employees to work hard and perform as they are expected to. Although emotional intelligence is one of the key skills of successful leaders in the corporate world, in this context leaders do not have the same

emotional connection to motivate their staff compared to the bond we have - or *can* have when we build it - with our children.

So given these strong parallels between parenting and leadership and despite the small differences, how can we use the best practice in parenting and leadership to help our children thrive? The objective of the following chapters is to answer this question.

Your Notes

CHAPTER 2

Becoming a Conscious & Strategic Parent

In corporate life we are used to defining a clear vision and strategy - whether for a whole business or for ourselves personally, as otherwise we wouldn't be maximising the chances of having a thriving business or being successful in our careers.

And yet, as parents, we are often 'reactive' - as opposed to strategic - in the way we deal with the challenges that our children 'throw' at us.

Becoming more 'strategic' in our approach to parenting is necessary because the majority of typical challenges - such as power struggles and arguments - can be prevented by anticipating situations and planning ahead. Taking a long-term view is essential because just like being successful in the workplace, becoming an effective parent isn't something that simply happens overnight; it is something that is built up slowly over time.

As parents, we may recognise on some level that what we are doing isn't working because the same situations keep repeating themselves over and over again. As a result, we are likely to become stuck in a pattern of behaviour, which may involve shouting and getting angry at our children out of frustration. This is particularly true for working parents who have even less time than stay-at-home parents to explore different ways to break out of these patterns.

In the corporate world, we recognise that there are different styles and approaches when it comes to leadership. Well, this is equally true of parenting. We can start breaking out of negative patterns of behaviour by identifying our individual style of parenting and understanding the strengths and weaknesses associated with that approach.

It is our job as parents to keep the bigger picture in mind and to equip our children with the tools they need to be able to deal with life's challenges. Indeed, kids' prefrontal cortex (the part of the brain that allows us to be rational and more strategic) is in development until the age of 25[4], and one of our key roles as parents is to help our children develop this prefrontal cortex as early as possible so that they make better choices and decisions in their lives.

This chapter focuses on how to think more strategically at home, so that we can become a more effective parent and find harmony and enjoyment in our everyday family lives. In it, we will share five tools that will help you to:

- Become more aware of the type of parent you are and the parent that you want to be.

- Become more strategic in your approach to parenting by gaining a better understanding of your child(ren).

- Learn to anticipate issues and power struggles before they arise.

  If you have a co-parent, these skills will allow you to work with your partner so that together, you can be the best possible parenting team.

TOOL #1
Understanding Your Strengths and Weaknesses

Objective: Becoming more aware of who you are as a parent so that you can utilise your strengths and become more confident and effective in your parenting approach.

"Accept yourself, your strengths, your weaknesses, your truths, and know what tools you have to fulfill your purpose."
Steve Maraboli, Best-Selling Author of Life, the Truth, and Being Free

In the corporate world, training is essential in ensuring that a team is able to perform well and carry out their duties to the best of their ability. Such training is expected in the workplace because it helps each team member to discover his or her individual strengths and weaknesses and their particular style of leadership. The awareness and tools that are acquired through this training allow each member of the team to reinforce their strengths and supplement their potential weaknesses, which makes for a more cohesive and productive working environment.

This is why companies invest billions of dollars in training, but of course the same cannot be said for parenting! As parents, we are tasked with the awesome responsibility of raising a child, without any real training or preparation at all. We are expected to know how to parent instinctively and the reality is that the only definite instincts that we have as parents are those of protection and nurturing. The other instincts that come to us are actually beliefs that we have learnt from our childhood[5], and we usually parent the way our parents parented us or in opposition to how we were parented.

Mollie (32, mother to Sasha, 8 and James 5) decides to attend an introduction to a parenting presentation given at her children's school.

The course leaders ask the attendees what they want to get out of the day, she answers: "I am a great mother and I have a great connection with my kids - most of the time. I am just here to see if there might be a few tricks and tips that could make my life as a single mother to two strong-willed children easier."

But as the session develops, she finds herself saying over and over:

"Oh, I'm not supposed to do that?"

"How on earth am I supposed to know that I'm not supposed to do this? This is what my parents used to do and it worked for me so why would it not work for my child?"

We need to develop our own way of parenting, as we are the ones who know our children better than anyone else and can best adapt our actions to their needs. So it's useful to understand our own individual style of parenting and our strengths and weaknesses. When we understand ourselves, only then can we truly begin to accept ourselves, for both our talents and our flaws. We are then able to start focusing on developing our talents by playing to our strengths, which allows us to 'make up for', and stop feeling guilty about, our weaknesses.

How to become a Leader parent

Suggestion 1: To get a better understanding of how you parent, spend 5 minutes reflecting on two questions:

1. "Who am I as a parent?"

    Thinking of qualities, such as the ones listed in the table below. Tick 5 qualities that you feel describe you best as a parent.
    Ask your partner - or a friend – if they agree with the qualities that you ticked.

2. "What qualities would I like to have more of as a parent?
    Thinking of qualities, such as the ones listed in the table below. Tick 5 qualities you'd like to display more of.

Parents Qualities

Parents Qualities	I am	I would like to be more
Accepting/Non-Judgemental	☐	☐
Calm	☐	☑
Confident/Assertive	☐	☐
Consistent	☐	☐
Creative	☐	☑
Dedicated	☐	☐
Demanding/Set high standards	☑	☐
Empathetic	☐	☐
Flexible	☐	☑
Fun/Playful	☐	☑
Gentle	☐	☐
Giving	☑	☐
Inspiring	☐	☐
Kind	☐	☐
Loving	☑	☐
Patient	☐	☑
Present	☐	☑
Organised	☑	☐
Persistent	☑	☐
Pro-active	☐	☐
Self-Aware	☐	☐
Setting clear rules	☐	☑
Supportive/Responsive	☐	☐
Understanding	☐	☐
Other:	☐	☐
....	☐	☐
....	☐	☐

Once you have done the above:

Choose one of the qualities that you want to be/have more of, then write it down somewhere you can see it regularly (e.g. on a post-it). Then for one week, practise exercising this quality as much as possible in your daily family life.

You'll start to become more conscious of when you're falling short of putting this quality into practice, which should help you to display this quality more often.

See the 5-Week Parenting Programme at the back of the book for more ideas of how to implement this.

Suggestion 2. The second suggestion is to learn more about the strengths and weaknesses of your 'default' parenting style. Although every parent is different, extensive academic research has shown that most parents typically adopt one of four styles[6]. Our intention is not to 'box' all parents with a definitive label because the reality is that many parents may adopt more than one parenting style. However, in moments of stress, the likelihood is that most parents will tend to fall into one of the categories detailed below, particularly when we are stressed and when our 'buttons are pushed' by our children. Below, we've included more information on the most common parenting styles, with a chart at the end that summarises the strengths and weaknesses of each style.

The Strict parent

The first parenting style is the 'Strict' parent, often referred to in the research as the 'Authoritarian' parent. Like any other parent, Strict parents want the best for their children. They tend to have high expectations of their kids and demand respect and obedience from them at all times. Strict parents often fear that their children may become spoilt or entitled, so they will tend to address disobedience or misbehaviour immediately with strict, 'logical', no-nonsense strategies. They are more likely to shout to ensure that their children obey them, and will usually resort to lectures and/or punishment to teach them a lesson.

This parenting style is often the result of having been raised this way themselves e.g. 'This is how my mum and dad raised me and I turned out ok, so why would I do things differently?'

The All-heart parent

The second parenting style is the 'All-heart' parent - sometimes referred to as the 'Permissive' parent - who is more indulgent, gentle, protective and usually has a more lenient attitude. All-heart parents tend to be very supportive of their children and believe that a loving connection should be maintained between parent and child at all times.

All-heart parents will have a tendency to want to protect their children from frustration, upset and disappointment. This protective tendency is why they will sometimes fall into the category of 'helicopter parents' who hover over their children to protect them from making mistakes.

For these parents, discipline is usually equal to punishment and to be avoided as much as possible, for fear that it may cause their child to feel upset or not feel loved. As a result, an All-heart parent can be prone to giving in to their child during conflict, which is often at the expense of setting clear limits for their child. These parents are typically the ones who are trying not to repeat their own parents' 'tough-love'/authoritarian parenting style - sometimes unconsciously, so they go to the other extreme.

How these styles affect children

Both of these 'typical' parenting styles tend to 'steal' from their children the opportunity to learn to solve problems by themselves, reducing their ability to become self-disciplined and responsible adults.

As the research shows[7], the Strict parents' insistence on obedience and control tends to damage the connection between parent and child, and it can create long-term resentment. Children of Strict parents might not always feel supported and loved because of the disconnection caused by harsh discipline, and it will usually result in more rebellion during adolescence. They also tend to be more vulnerable to the pressures of peer groups because they're not used to thinking for themselves and taking responsibility for their own behaviour.

The All-heart parent often gives their children the message - without realising it - that disappointment, frustration and other upsetting emotions must be avoided at all cost. The lack of boundary setting makes it harder for their kids to manage their emotions and to bounce back, which is essential to developing resilience. What sometimes amounts to 'overprotection' can create a sense of entitlement from the child, and can lead to resentment and dependency towards the parent and others in the long-term[8].

Both styles in the extreme disempower their children. All-heart parents disempower their children by over-protecting them, while Strict parents disempower their children by 'over-control' through the use of orders and discipline. Unfortunately, children who feel disempowered are more likely to misbehave and enter into conflict and power struggles with their parents.

Compensation Strategies

To further complicate family life, couples often have different parenting styles and the family dynamic becomes more fraught when each partner detects 'failings' in the other's parenting style and starts over compensating as a result. In this situation, parents often find themselves operating at the other extreme of the parenting scale - being even more permissive where the other parent is being too strict and vice versa. Perhaps the ultimate irony is the fact that children often turn this 'schism' between their parents to their advantage, using the frequent disagreements as leverage to get what they want. If this sounds familiar, read Tool #2 - **Teamwork** to find solutions to this common challenge.

The Uncertain parent

Given the stress of modern family life and uncertainty as to which parenting style is the most effective, many parents find themselves fluctuating between being strict and having a more permissive/over-protecting approach. The approach that they adopt largely depends on their mood, level of stress, feelings of guilt for not spending enough time with their children, and the 'association' that each situation holds for them, which is usually related to their childhood.

Whether we overcompensate for our absence by being too lenient, or take a short cut to instilling good behaviour by being too strict, children are likely to sense our underlying dissatisfaction with our own behaviour. This contradiction can create confusion and frustration for our children and additional stress for us parents too.

This style of parenting is different from being a 'Balanced parent' (see below). In the majority of cases, it makes it more difficult for children to be responsible and self-disciplined because the parents' reactions lack consistency and are not always congruent for the child. As a result, the children do not know whether they will be dealing with our nice/more permissive side or our stricter/harsher side. This is why it is so important to have more balance as a parent and avoid oscillating from one extreme to another.

The Leader parent – Aka The Balanced parent

The fourth style, the style of parenting we aspire to, is what we call 'Balanced' - also called Authoritative in some of the research.

As this book combines the best practice in leadership and parenting, we will call Balanced parents, Leader parents.

These parents take a broader and more balanced view than their more 'extreme' counterparts. However, it's not just about finding a happy medium between being strict and being indulgent.

Leader parents provide children with good boundaries and set high expectations, while being supportive. They encourage family discussion and critical thinking, and allow their children to develop self-reliance, a healthy level of self-esteem and a sense of responsibility.

They establish rules and guidelines and hold their children accountable for their actions. Yet, rather than resorting to punitive discipline, they use empathy and a strong connection with their child as a basis for their authority.

The Leader style reconciles the strengths and limitations of each of the other styles - borrowing the more positive elements while ironing out the negative - to deliver the best possible experience to their children, in the short as well as in the longer term. And as well as improved behaviour, children who are empowered by parents who adopt this style tend to score highly in self-esteem and emotional intelligence tests[9].

Strengths and Weaknesses of each parenting style

Parenting Style	Strengths	Weaknesses
Strict/ Authoritarian	- Gets things done - Persistent - Assertive - Imposes rules - Clear direction - Usually more organised	- Rigid: develops less closeness, creativity, spontaneity - Often overinvolved - Uses power to impose discipline: This is likely to make this parent have less influence over time ✶ **Negative effects on children:** - They will not always feel supported and loved - They will usually obey the rules out of fear rather than learning to be self-reliant - Can lead them to become more aggressive, particularly if they've been hit and/or shamed - They will often develop resentment in the long run and are more likely to rebel and become 'overly irresponsible' either at adolescence or when leaving home to make up for the rule enforcement
All Heart/ Over-protective	- Empathetic - Makes fewer demands - Develops closeness and connection - Able to compromise - Non-aggressive - Usually encourages more creativity	- Doesn't set enough limits/boundaries - Doesn't take enough care of self - Often overinvolved - Will tend to be too sympathetic - as opposed to just being empathetic - which can reinforce certain negative behaviours **Negative effects on children:** - They may become entitled, self-centred and anxious - They develop less ability to cope with frustration and challenges of life, so they are less resilient - They can become 'praise junkies' - so dependent on approval that they lack self-reliance ✶ - They will often develop resentment in the long-run, even though this type of parent may have seemed like the 'perfect parent' when they were growing up

Parenting Style	Strengths	Weaknesses
Uncertain	Depending on the style they adopt the majority of the time, they will develop some of the skills relating to that parenting style.	- Swings from one approach to another (strict in one situation and permissive in another) - Lacks consistency - Doesn't set clear expectations -Tendency to doubt oneself **Negative effects on children:** - They can develop anxiety as the lack of consistency in parenting style makes them always wonder which 'type' of parent they are going to encounter - Makes it more difficult for them to control their emotions and be consistent - because the parent, who is their model, is not clear in their expectations - Can lead to self-doubt as they are unsure of the 'right' way to behave because their parent's expectations of them are always changing
Leader	**Develops in children:** - Happiness - Good boundaries - Self-discipline - Responsibility - Emotional Intelligence - Resilience - Self-esteem	Parents who manage to achieve this balance might be striving to be the 'perfect' parent, which is unrealistic and could be counterproductive.

 TOOL #2
Teamwork

NB: *This tool is written for couples, but it also applies to single parents whose ex-partner is still involved in raising their child.*

Objective: *Creating more harmony in couples and the family and increasing cooperation with other carers*

> *"Teamwork is the ability to work together toward a common vision."*
> **Andrew Carnegie, 19th Century Industrialist**

> *"Coming together is a beginning.*
> *Keeping together is progress. Working together is success."*
> **Henry Ford, Founder of the Ford Motoring Company**

Teamwork is the basis of good management and leadership. This is even truer when two leaders need to work together to manage a team. Co-managers who agree on expectations and send consistent messages are far more likely to be able to drive their business towards long-term success.

One of the most common challenges that parents face is finding that their own individual style of parenting is at odds with that of their partner's, and they can end up becoming locked in a 'good cop vs bad cop' pattern. What often makes things worse is that parents end up operating in 'compensation strategies' (see Tool #1 - **Understanding Your Strengths and Weaknesses**).

When two parents are unable to find common ground and disagree on how to deal with typical parenting challenges, the strength of the family unit as a whole is diminished. And if children are on the receiving end of mixed messages from their parents, this can be extremely confusing. How are they to know what is expected of them and how to react if their parents can't work as a team and agree on a parenting strategy?

Jack (44, married to Anna, 42, parents of Peter, 14, Kirsty, 8 and Chloe, 6) calls his wife from the train: "Great leadership course today, amazing insights. I'll be home soon, I hope the kids will have done their homework by then."

As Jack comes back home and sees his kids playing on the iPad, he asks Anna:

"Great, the kids have finished their homework then?"

"Not yet", she replied.

"Then why are you letting them play on the iPad?! I thought we'd agreed that the rule was that they had to finish their homework before they get any screen time?"

"I know what we agreed, but they've had a really tough few days at school and they wouldn't stop pestering me, so I thought where's the harm? After all, they could do with having a bit of fun."

"What's the point in us making an agreement if you're just going to undermine me? The kids are going to become spoilt brats if you keep giving in to them."

"But we'll lose the connection we have with them if you keep shouting at them and losing your temper all the time!"

The children who were watching them mumble: "Here they go, fighting again". They go to another room to continue watching their screens.

How to become a Leader parent

Parenting is without a doubt, the ultimate 'teamwork' and requires a lot of tolerance and patience, especially if both parents are equally involved.

Just as we need to try to work in harmony with our colleagues in order to run a successful business, it's also important to work alongside our co-parent - if we have one - and be consistent in our parenting approach if we wish to create a happy and harmonious family life. Being inconsistent in our approach and expectations invariably leads to conflict with our children and disagreements with our spouse, as Jack and Anna are clearly experiencing in the scenario described above.

It's also important to remember that kids pick up on far more than parents realise; they can sense if there's a fracture or weak spot in the family unit, and this can affect their behaviour in a number of ways. They are likely to exploit the fact that their parents can't agree by playing one parent against the other.

That's why it is so important to be more 'strategic' in our approach to parenting, and to discuss potential issues with our partner before they arise to prevent disagreements and arguments from happening in front of our children.

How to use Teamwork:

1. Start by having a conversation with your spouse/partner or co-parent in which you discuss:

   a) What your hopes are for your children and what you want them to become.

   b) What your default parenting styles are likely to be. Ideally, you should do this after both completing the exercise 'Who am I as a parent?' in the preceding Tool #1 - **Understanding Your Strengths and Weaknesses**.

   c) Agree with your partner what your 'core' values are, for example, good manners, tidiness or spending quality family time together (see Tool #14 - **Family Culture**).

   d) Then decide what you both consider to be acceptable and unacceptable behaviour based on these principles. This enables you to set household rules that are clear and accepted by everyone (see Tool #11 - **Setting Rules**).

   e) The above exercise is likely to leave areas where you might disagree and this is fine as it is almost impossible to reach an agreement on everything. You will need to both agree to be flexible in these instances and to be accepting of these differences.

2. Make an agreement with your partner, that so long as you are both maintaining these shared values and rules, you will allow each other room to express your individual parenting styles and you will stop blaming each other for your weaknesses.

3. If there are tensions surrounding certain household tasks (bedtime routine, bath time etc.), then divide them. Agree on 'territories' that you will each need to commit to respecting. The key thing is to both play to your strengths, thereby reducing friction simply by agreeing on the tasks you will each do and ensuring that you stick to the plan.

4. Don't compensate for your spouses' parenting style. So for example, if your spouse has a more lenient approach to parenting, be aware that you will probably have a tendency to compensate by becoming stricter and this will only serve to undermine their authority and make them feel unsupported.

5. Avoid taking sides with your child and/or sabotaging your partner's actions, and don't allow your child to manipulate you into conflict with your partner. For example if a child says, "But Mum/Dad always lets me stay up late!" (most kids will try this at some point or another!), answer, "He/She may well do, but right now I'm the one who's responsible for looking after you".

   And for single parents, try adapting this answer slightly by saying: "I hear that your Mum/Dad may do things differently, but in this house, this is how we do things". Children need to learn that there may be different sets of rules in different environments and they are usually ok with it as long as we are consistent.

6. It is important to try to be as consistent as possible when it comes to applying these tools and whatever parenting strategy agreed upon with your partner. Consistency is difficult, because as human beings it is in our nature to have moments where we just want to relax and not have to give too much thought to our actions or behaviour. However, it's always important to ensure that you send a clear message to your child

so that they know where the boundaries are and they don't get confused by mixed messages.

7. If and when you disagree with your partners' reactions to your child's misbehaviour, avoid intervening or expressing this in front of your child as otherwise you send the message to your co-parent that they are incapable of dealing with the situation. If you feel your partner is starting to lose their temper and think there may be a better way to deal with the situation, try asking, "Can I help?". However, if their answer is "No", then do respect this.

8. If you find it too difficult not to intervene, and particularly if you are getting angry, it's much better to remove yourself from the situation by leaving the room rather than allowing the disagreement to escalate. Otherwise, children will sense the tension and this can have quite a detrimental effect on their wellbeing.

9. If you feel the issue is still unresolved, discuss this with your partner later on when your child isn't present. This may involve talking about how you could have handled things differently and identifying how to deal with the situation in a more effective way, should it arise again.

10. Model conflict resolution: sometimes despite our best intentions, we can find ourselves disagreeing and arguing with our spouse in front of our children. In an ideal world, find an amicable solution in their presence, so they learn how to deal with conflict rather than fear it. This is also important, because if children don't see the resolution they could be left with a sense of anxiety about what has happened. However, if there is too much tension to resolve things, it is better to agree to discuss this later – and either one of you can leave the room if necessary - rather than let the argument flare up.

11. Think about your children's relationships with other carers such as relatives, child-minders and nannies. Clarifying your wishes and expectations to these other carers and sharing some of the tools in this book will help prevent other carers from inadvertently undermining your efforts when you're

not around (see the end of the 5-Week Programme where there is a specific programme for carers). However, while consistency between different carers makes things easier, it is not a requisite because children understand that different people will treat them in different ways. As long as both parents are as consistent in their approach as possible, then it doesn't matter quite so much if other carers do things differently.

12. Finally, make sure that you celebrate your partner for improvements in how he/she is dealing with your child - even if they seem insignificant to you - and show appreciation for the efforts that they are making. This is the best way to get rid of the blame and make this a positive self-reinforcing cycle.

✖ TOOL #3
Understanding Your Children

Objective: Gaining a better understanding of children's individual needs and temperament

> *"You have to look at leadership through the eyes*
> *of the followers and you have to live the message.*
> *I have learned that people become motivated when you guide*
> *them to the source of their own power."*
> **Anita Roddick, Founder of The Body Shop**

> *"I believe the real difference between success and failure*
> *in a corporation can be very often traced to the question*
> *of how well the organization brings out the great*
> *energies and talents of its people."*
> **Thomas J. Watson, Jr., Former Chairman and CEO of IBM**

One of the keys to being a successful leader in the workplace is recognising and understanding the needs of colleagues and/or team members. Doing this helps each member of the team feel valued so they are more likely to be responsive and comply with any requests that are made of them. And team members who feel respected and valued are motivated to fulfil their potential and become the best they can be.

Similarly, as parents, we are tasked with the awesome (and rather scary!) responsibility of ensuring that our children's potential is being realised. It is only once we allow ourselves the time to tune into our child's unique temperament and become aware of their key needs – beyond the basic needs for food and shelter - that we can help prevent misbehaviour, and use the connection we have built with them as the base of our influence 'over' them.

There are many models and theories about human needs. William Glasser's five key needs described in his Theory of Choice[10] is a simple and powerful model to identify the key needs in both work and family life. According to Glasser, the five key human needs are: Freedom and Autonomy, Power & Significance, Love & Belonging, Fun & Play and Survival (basic needs for food, shelter, etc.).

Adapted from William Glasser's Theory of Choice

All of these key human needs have to be met in order for a person to be happy and fulfilled. Our children are hugely dependent on us to fulfil these needs, and we can fall short of addressing them – usually without realising it. These unmet needs are usually the reason behind our children 'mis'behaviour.

A prime example of this is children's need for Freedom and Autonomy and Power and Significance, which is closely linked to their need to have a sense of control over their lives. This need for control and asserting their own identity increases around the age of two (which helps explain the terrible twos!), and then again around adolescence. And yet, children rarely get a say, particularly when they are very young.

This alone is at the origin of most power struggles and other family challenges. Parent and child can get stuck into a head to head where one needs to win at the expense of the other. This leads to a negative cycle where the child feels that they have even less control over their lives and will end up being even less cooperative.

That is not to say that we need to give children unrestricted control and allow them to run the family, as can sometimes happen in households where both parents are more indulgent. As we will see in Chapter 2, there are ways to give a child the impression of control in a way that meets their needs and to do so on our terms.

Another key example of this is when a child starts mis-behaving, we can become caught in a downward spiral of getting angry, lecturing and punishing. Such power struggles are an entirely negative experience for the child (see Tool #19 - **Logical and Delayed Consequences**), so it will not allow them to fulfil their needs for Love and Belonging and Power and Significance and will usually end up making the situation worse.

What we can learn from research and neuroscience

1. Why our children do not always seem rational

Our children's 'consciousness' is not fully developed until the age of 10 or 11 and their prefrontal cortex is in development until the age of 25[11]. The latter is the part of the brain that allows us to be rational and more strategic because it influences 'executive functions' such as planning and impulse control. This means that children cannot be as aware of the consequences of their mistakes as an adult is, and they will often make decisions without fully comprehending the consequences of their actions.

This also means that their 'mis'behaviour, rather than an attempt to manipulate us or be spiteful, is actually a sort of 'teasing things out' to see what works. Children behave in this way because they think they will meet some of their needs for power and significance, freedom and autonomy or love and belonging.

During adolescence, the consequence of this lack of full development of the prefrontal cortex and the increased activity of the brain's 'reward function' (i.e. giving more importance to instant pleasures) is that adolescents usually take more risks than their parents would deem 'rational'[12]. This increase in risk-taking behaviour means that this part of development often proves to be a particularly challenging period.

This is why one of our key roles as parents is to help our kids develop their pre-frontal cortex early on. In doing this, we enable them to better understand the consequences of their actions, deal with frustration and be able to delay gratification, and subsequently, make better choices in life. Many of the tools in this book are aimed at achieving this.

2. Why our children often don't listen to us

As human beings, we move toward what is pleasurable and move away from what is not. We are hardwired for protection so our brains instantly respond to signals of threat and we move away to protect ourselves. What this means for our relationships with our children, is that conversations that feel threatening to them - loud, accusing or angry, cause the child on the receiving end, to retreat, resist, and recoil from engagement[13].

It is therefore essential, to use communication techniques such as the ones described in **Chapter 2** to ensure that our children don't feel threatened by us and make them feel safe to listen to us and talk to us. It's important to try to notice when we are sending threatening signals and refocus, redirect and reframe instead.

3. Why our children get stressed when we are stressed

Neuroscientists have only recently discovered that humans have 'mirror neurons', which can explain the capacity of humans to be empathetic[14]. These mirror neurons also explain why emotions and feelings are contagious: when we are stressed, people around us tend to become stressed as well, and when we experience emotions such as sadness and joy, these emotions are likely to also have an effect on people around us.

4. Why our children cannot learn when we shout or get angry

Most of the time, we shout at our children because we are trying to teach them a valuable lesson and/or stop them from misbehaving. For example, when we tell them in a loud voice 'Calm down!', 'Stop immediately!' or 'Stop Crying!', we may think that we are appealing to their logical side by showing them that what they are doing is making us angry and that they should therefore stop. However, neuroscience shows that quite the opposite is true, and that we are actually making it more difficult for them to control their actions and emotions.

Indeed, when we shout at our children, rather than appealing to their logical side, which is located in the prefrontal cortex, we are instead creating a 'fight or flight' or 'freeze' response from the body. This accelerates their nervous system and stimulates their limbic system (also called 'The Chimp' in a well-known mind management book[15]). This results is an increased production of hormones such as Cortisol, which is also known as the 'anxiety hormone'). Once Cortisol is in the body, it usually takes time to eliminate it so the body is likely to stay in a state of stress and anxiety for some time.

This physiological response means that children become unable to process most of what we tell them (think of the lectures that we often try to give our children while they are in this state?), which makes it harder for them to calm down or stop crying.

Worse still, when children do not learn to manage their intense feelings while they're young, they become more prone to over-react to 'minor stressors' in life and become anxious, or angry for much of the time[16].

Extensive scientific research shows that a child's quality of life is dramatically affected by whether or not we help them establish effective stress-regulating systems and anti-anxiety chemical systems.

So it is vital for parents to learn how to react differently and to regulate their own emotions.

5. Why rewards don't work in the long run

Children are born with an 'intrinsic motivation' to do things to the best of their ability, to please their parents and to get along well with others[17]. When children engage in a task or activity for the sheer joy of taking part, this is because they are intrinsically motivated to do so. Research shows that if a child is offered 'extrinsic motivation' such as money, sticker charts or even praise, this external incentive can supersede their intrinsic motivation to do well for themselves [18].

Over time, these rewards often become a child's prime motivator for putting effort into something, whether it be taking on a new challenge, completing homework or a chore or even when it comes to participating in an activity that they enjoy. In other words, when we offer them a reward or incentive for their efforts, their attention is taken away from the activity and is focused on the reward instead. So when we remove the reward, our children's motivation to do well is likely to disappear with it.

What's more, research shows that people taught to act in the expectation of extrinsic rewards turn out to be less happy and less successful, and to have less satisfying relationships than those who are internally motivated[19].

Using rewards and bribes (such as sweets, ice cream, etc.) to relieve children from upset and frustration is also counter-productive, as it doesn't allow them to learn to control their emotions (refer to Tool #17 - **Emotion Coaching**).

Finally, the biggest danger is that we may find that our children become increasingly reluctant to do anything we ask of them because they will always be asking, "What's my reward for doing as I'm told?". The other big issue is that these rewards are likely to get bigger and bigger as our children grow and are bound to create some serious negotiations, which we can prevent by using more effective techniques such as the tools provided in this book.

Julia (28) and John (30) are with their child Annabelle (3) at the supermarket and she is having a tantrum:

Julia finds herself starting to lose her temper and raises her voice:

"Annabelle, you need to stop that silly behaviour right now or I'm going to get really cross with you.

Annabelle is in tears by this stage and starts screaming even louder.

"You don't need to shout at her Julia, you're making things worse!" John says, aware that the other people in the supermarket are starting to stare. John cannot stand seeing Annabelle so miserable so he gets close to her and gently says:

"I'll tell you what, if you help Mummy and me put the shopping in the basket without making a fuss, I'll buy you an ice cream at the checkout. How about that?"

Annabelle's outburst stops in an instant; 'What's next on your list Mummy?'.

As Annabelle is happily eating her ice cream in the back of the car, it is dripping on the floor, so Julia shouts at her: "Watch it Annabelle, the ice cream is dripping all over the car seat, quickly give it to me!"

Annabelle 'freezes' at her mother's panicky shouting. She ends up dropping the ice cream and starts to scream again.

How to become a Leader parent

An effective leader understands the motivation behind the behaviour of those he/she is trying to lead. Jack and Anna would have had an entirely different experience at the supermarket if they had a better understanding of Annabelle's key needs and didn't make it harder for her to regulate her emotions. In other words, if our children are failing to meet our expectations, then it's up to us to:

1. Take the time to get to know our children in a deeper way. Working with our child's personality, we need to learn to develop their individual traits and abilities, and sometimes

temper strengths that, left unchecked, could become a liability. For example, an assertive, outgoing personality is a great trait in a leader, but without self-control, it can be seen as overly aggressive and controlling.

2. Identify whether it is our expectation that is creating the issue. We sometimes forget to check whether our expectations are 'normal' and age appropriate and this is a delicate balancing act. You need to keep in mind the development of the brain as explained above and there are great books on the subject. Most of the tools in this book are meant to better understand your child and meet their needs so they will enable you to adapt your expectations to your child's.

3. When misbehaviour occurs, we should look for the reasons behind the misbehaviour, which is often that one of one of our child's needs is not being addressed. Use the tools in this book to ensure optimal communication and find effective solutions to the misbehaviour that will fulfil your children's needs. Here is a list of the specific tools in this book that address each of the key needs:

- **Survival:** We assume that parents reading this book are meeting their children's needs for 'survival', i.e. shelter, food, etc. But when they are infants and toddlers, remember to follow your child's cues for food, rest, play and comfort as these are often the reasons behind their misdeeds.

- **Freedom and Autonomy**: Planning Ahead - Tool #4, Creating Routines - Tool #5, Limited Choices - Tool #6, Asking Questions - Tool #7, Emotion Coaching - Tool #17, Mistakes as Opportunities for Learning - Tool #18, Growth Mindset - Tool #20, Problem Solving - Tool #21

- **Power and Significance:** Limited Choices - Tool #6, Asking Questions - Tool #7, Positive Redirection - Tool #9, Effective Communication - Tool #10, Family Contribution - Tool #15, Mistakes as Opportunities for Learning - Tool #18, Growth Mindset - Tool #20, Problem Solving – Tool #21, Family Meetings - Tool #22

- **Love and Belonging**: Limited Choices - Tool #6, Effective Communication – Tool #10, Leading by Example - Tool #12, Family Culture - Tool #14, Presence - Tool #16, Emotion Coaching - Tool #17, Growth Mindset – Tool #20, Family Meetings - Tool #22

- **Fun and Play**: Once you've applied the tools above, you will have saved a lot of time in useless power struggles and stress, so you will have much more time to have fun and play with your kids!

⊗ TOOL #4
Planning Ahead

Objective: Anticipating issues and power struggles before they arise by becoming more strategic

"Failing to plan is planning to fail."
Alan Lakein, Best-Selling Author of
'How to Get Control of Your Time and Your Life'

In corporate life, having the ability to anticipate potential problems *before* they happen, and knowing how to minimise any damage caused on the occasions when problems do occur is a key leadership skill and makes everyday life in the workplace so much easier.

Many of the everyday challenges that parents face can be prevented by being more 'strategic' and anticipating potential trouble and conflict before it happens. This isn't always easy when we are trying to juggle work with family life; when we are stressed, overworked or tired, we are far more likely to react to our children's 'mis'behaviour rather than respond to it. In these circumstances, we often end up telling off our children - and potentially sending them into 'fight of flight' (see Tool #3 - **Understanding Your Children**), instead of teaching them valuable lessons.

Mollie is about to take Sasha (8) to swimming class, but yet again, they're running late:

"Come on Sasha, would you please hurry up, we should have left ten minutes ago!"

"But I can't find my swimming costume."

"Well, you clearly weren't looking very hard – look, it's right here in your wardrobe. You must have put it there by mistake as it's usually in your drawer. Have you packed your goggles and a clean towel?"

"No, not yet."

"I take you swimming every single week, surely you must know what you need to take with you by now?!"

Another ten minutes pass, and Sasha is still ambling around looking for her swimming goggles, while Mollie waits at the front door tapping her foot loudly against the floor...

Taking the time to plan ahead by anticipating the needs of different situations and our children's reactions can significantly reduce power struggles and prevent a lot of time wasted in whining, arguing and negotiating.

How to become a Leader parent

Children like to know in advance what is going to happen and to be 'involved' wherever possible as this helps to give them a sense of control over the situation. They're also more likely to comply with a request or behave as they have been asked to if they have already agreed to it in advance.

How to plan ahead:

1. **Identify the main issues** that tend to cause conflict or lead to a power struggle with your child.

2. **Think about what you could do in advance** to improve things when a challenging situation should present itself again. For example, in Mollie's example above, she could:

   a) Ensure Sasha prepares the swimming bag in advance and that the swimming clothes are always in the same place.

   b) Involve her daughter Sasha in creating a routine so that she knows exactly what she needs to be doing every week before going swimming or any other regular task (see Tool #5 - **Creating Routines**).

3. **Create pre-agreements**: tell your child what is likely to happen and when (for example if they are going to the doctors), and if necessary create an agreement on how you are going

to cope with any challenging situations you are likely to encounter.

These pre-agreements are very useful for anything that involves going out of the house such as play-dates, for being polite (saying "Hello" and "Thank You") or if you are planning a trip to the supermarket. Here are the key steps for a pre-agreement prior to a trip to the supermarket:

a) The first step is to sit down with your child(ren) and agree what the boundaries are, and then make an agreement about how you'd like them to behave during the trip. Make the agreement as specific as possible - this may include whether they can expect a treat, or whether you expect them to help out. Then use a **Positive & Enforceable Statement** (see Tool #8) such as: "I take children to the supermarket who do not whine and keep asking me to buy them things." This is much more effective than a vague statement and a threat such as: "If you don't behave, I won't take you to the supermarket."

b) Once you've made the agreement, you can ensure that they understand what is expected of them by asking them to repeat what has been agreed. If they aren't able to repeat everything, try nudging them with a short reminder, "And the next step is?". Being able to visualise themselves performing the task helps a child to store it in their long-term memory.

c) Ask your child how they would like to be reminded in the event that they break part of their agreement. This will give them a chance to 'redirect' their behaviour without you having to leave the supermarket in case they make a mistake (which is likely to happen!).

d) If your child is older than three, you can even include them in deciding what the logical consequence should be if the agreement isn't adhered to. For example, you may agree with your kids that if they pester you for sweets, you'll have to leave the supermarket straight away (if this is viable for you) or simply that you won't be buying anything for them.

NB: These suggestions, like others in this book, may sound time-consuming. But by becoming more strategic through planning ahead and applying these suggestions, you will be saving a lot of time in the long run. And, as you continue to use this tool and others, you will become more skilled at it, as will the children, and it will become second nature and much easier to implement.

Further examples for solving typical parenting challenges

1. Morning Issues: Taking too long to do everything

If your kids are taking too long to do everything, it's useful to think about what you can do in advance to help them speed things up. For example, you could give them **Limited Choices** (Tool #6) of what they would like to wear the night before and lay them out ready to put on in the morning, or you could try waking them up a little earlier.

2. Tantrums

The primary causes of tantrums are tiredness, hunger, lack of activity, or sudden changes in environment. By planning ahead and anticipating these potential issues, and having a plan in place in case they occur, you can significantly reduce the likelihood of tantrums happening in the first place.

3. Teaching values such as politeness

Before going to your relative's house, agree with your child(ren) how they should behave at your relatives and what the rules are. For example, you could ask them: "What are we supposed to do when we arrive there? And what about when they serve us cakes?" Once your child agrees to this, they are much more likely to comply. And you can also agree on a gentle 'secret' reminder in case they forget that will not shame them in front of others.

⚙ TOOL #5
Creating Routines

Objective: *Equipping children with invaluable life-skills such as planning and organisation and increasing their cooperation*

> *"The only possible way to have it all is with structure and the discipline to keep to it, to make it a routine."*
> **Margot Hattingh, South African Artist**

One of the most effective ways of improving performance of a specific task is through structure and repetition. When routines are in place, people know exactly what they are supposed to be doing and at what time and clearly understand what is expected of them, which allows them to function and perform more efficiently in their jobs. And when managing a team at work, the team leader will naturally involve the whole team in setting a schedule and ask them for feedback to help ensure that everyone is 'on the same page' and that the schedule that is put in place is working effectively.

In family life, our children are expected to perform lots of tasks and follow many routines from waking up, brushing teeth, washing hands, taking a bath, etc. as well as other household tasks/chores on a daily basis. However, there isn't always a clear structure and a clear expectation of the time such tasks should take in place, and usually children are not involved in setting these routines.

Also, we often end up repeating ourselves and nagging them about what they should be doing, which ends up making them less responsible for doing it. And as a result, they'll wait for us to say things several times before actually doing what we have asked.

Anna is trying to get her daughter, Chloe (6), to arrive at school on time – she's been late almost every day for the last week because she's taking ages to get dressed every morning.

As Chloe eats her breakfast, Anna says:

"Chloe, can you please eat up your breakfast, we can't be late again this morning."

Chloe continues to eat at a snail's pace.

"Did you not hear me, Chloe? Would you please eat your breakfast, we're going to be late if you don't hurry up."

When she's finally finished, Anna ushers her into the bedroom to get her dressed.

"Would you please hurry up, Chloe! You haven't even washed your face or cleaned your teeth yet!"

Chloe doesn't appear to be taking much notice, so Anna repeats herself:

"How many more time do I have to say it? Hurry up, Chloe! We're already running late, now wash your hands and brush your teeth so that we can go! I will not tell you again!"

Anna hovers over Chloe to try to speed her up any way she can, but to no avail, and all the while the seconds keep ticking by...

Children often procrastinate without any apparent reason, but wouldn't a lot of us procrastinate as well if we knew that someone would be there to remind us several times over of what we were supposed to do next?

How to become a Leader parent

Although children may appear to dislike routines on the surface, the reality is that they need some form of 'systematic approach' in their everyday life, particularly when they are young. Routines help to give children a sense of stability and security and help them to understand how to behave and what is expected of them.

As their prefrontal cortex is not fully developed, it is totally normal for them to struggle much more than adults with time management and impulse control. It is therefore key to coach them to develop their time-management skills and to use the routine as an opportunity for learning, rather than disempower them by constantly nagging and reminding them.

Involving them in the process of building their daily routines is a great way of empowering them and enables the routine to 'become the boss' rather than us, which significantly increases the child's cooperation. Involving them in creating their daily schedule also helps to develop a child's sense of self-responsibility and improves their organisational skills, and makes them less inclined to want to enter into negotiations and power struggles.

How to create routines:

1. Identify the type of recurring tasks (e.g. in the morning or in the evening), which can be broken down into a sequence of steps.

2. Discuss with your child what the routine or steps are that they need to go through in order to complete the task. It's ideal to do this brainstorming session during a **Family Meeting** (Tool #22). For example, devise a 'going to sleep' ritual with your child. This evening ritual might include: bath, brushing teeth, getting into pyjamas, reading story (a prayer, poem or lullaby often helps calm a child), lights out.

3. Once you have identified these steps, make a visual guide to this routine using photos of each step. Or alternatively, if your child is able to draw, a drawing to illustrate each step, and if they are able to write, they can make their own list.

4. Include the amount of time each of the steps should take, or the time at which the routine needs to end by (as the objective is that the task is to be completed by an agreed time). When they are younger than five, they do not yet have a clear sense of time so you can be the time-keeper or you can use a sand timer.

5. With your child's help, arrange the pictures (or drawings) into a sequence on a chart, then peg or glue them on and include the timings underneath.

6. Ask your child how they would like to be reminded in the event that they find themselves struggling to follow the schedule as agreed. For example, they might want you to ask them: "What does *your* schedule say you should do next?"

NB: If they initially struggle with these schedules, try doing a 'think through' with them by asking: "Can you run me through your morning schedule?" And then as they go through it, simply nudge them with a short question, "And what is the next step?". This helps them to visualise and remember their routine, which will help them to incorporate it into their long-term memory.

How to Become a Conscious & Strategic Parent

- Identify your individual parenting style and think about the strengths and weaknesses associated with that style.

- Focus on developing your talents by playing to your strengths as a parent.

- Try to be as consistent as possible in your individual parenting style - rather than fluctuating between being strict and lenient- so that your children understand what is expected of them.

- Become more strategic in your approach to parenting by discussing potential issues with your partner before they arise.

- Decide with your partner what your shared core values are, then make an agreement that so long as you are both maintaining these shared values, you will allow each other room to express your individual parenting styles.

- Think about ways to address children's key needs for Freedom and Autonomy, Power and Significance, Love and Belonging and Fun and Play. Fulfilling these needs will increase their cooperation and help you to build a strong sense of trust and connection with them.

- Remember that shouting and getting angry makes it more difficult for a child to comply with any requests that are made of them as they go into 'fight or flight'.

- Identify the main issues that tend to cause conflict or lead to a power struggle with your child and think in advance about what steps you could take to prevent this from happening – remember, planning is prevention.

- Always tell children exactly what is going to happen and when as this helps to give them a sense of control over the situation - they like to know in advance what is going to happen and to be 'involved' wherever possible.

- Build a daily routine to give children a sense of stability and security, which will make them less inclined to want to enter into negotiations and power struggles.

- Involve children as much as possible in creating their daily routines as this helps to develop their sense of self-responsibility.

Your Notes

CHAPTER 3

Communicating Effectively to Meet Children's Needs

In corporate life, significant efforts are made to communicate effectively with colleagues and fellow team members because it helps to promote a more cohesive and productive working environment. In family life, we seldom use the same 'communication tools' that we use with our colleagues in the workplace.

We need to get our children to do so many things on a daily basis, and the most common way to get them to do these things is by issuing an order/command - even if it starts with 'please do this' or 'please don't do that'. In fact, research shows that the average parent gives their child a staggering 34 commands every hour on average[20], often without even realising it!

Any adult would become resistant to cooperating if they were given this many commands every hour, and as parents, we often forget that children have very similar needs to us. In recognising this, we can begin to understand why our demands of them often provoke so much resistance and opposition. The most effective way to improve communication and increase our children's willingness to cooperate with us is by finding alternatives to commands, threats, nagging and reminding as all of these serve to undermine their key needs.

The tools in this chapter are designed to help you:

• Communicate effectively
• Fulfil your child's key needs
• Increase cooperation
• Improve the family dynamic

⊗ TOOL #6
Limited Choices

Objective: Increasing cooperation by fulfilling children's need for autonomy and control

"Control leads to compliance; autonomy leads to engagement."
Daniel H. Pink, Best-Selling Author of 'Drive:
The Surprising Truth About What Motivates Us'

"One's philosophy is expressed in the choices one makes…
and the choices we make are ultimately our responsibility."
Eleanor Roosevelt, American politician, Diplomat, & Activist

In the workplace, people feel much more valued if they are asked their opinion and given choices rather than simply being told what to do. This key leadership skill encourages colleagues/team members to be more cooperative because it fulfils their need for autonomy, control and belonging and it therefore ensures that they remain motivated.

As parents, we need to get our children to do so many things on a daily basis, so we spend a lot of time telling them what to do and making decisions on their behalf. We may think that this is the only way of ensuring that they do what they need to do on time, but the reality is that children don't like to be ordered around and told what to do any more than we adults do. Children, like all human beings, have a need for control and autonomy (see Tool #3 - **Understanding Your Children**). So not surprisingly, their reaction to orders and commands is often negative, such as not cooperating, ignoring us, arguing or even anger turned inwards in the form of resentment.

Chloe (6) is busy playing with her toys in the living room, when Jack walks into the room and says:

"Chloe, you need to put your toys away now and wash your hands because dinner is in ten minutes."

"But I'm still playing! I don't want to wash my hands – can't I just eat my dinner later?"

"No you can't, now do as you are told and put your toys away. I'll be back in five minutes to check on you."

Five minutes pass, and Jack checks on Chloe, who is still happily playing.

"Dinner is served and you haven't even started tidying up your toys, let alone washed your hands! Why don't you ever listen to me or do as you're told!"

How to become a Leader parent

To help encourage children to be more autonomous and give them the impression that they have some control over their lives, it's important to try to avoid simply telling them what to do. One of the most effective alternatives to orders/commands is to offer them Limited Choices (both of which suit the parent). So for example, we can ask our child "Would you rather wear this coat or this one?" instead of "Please put your coat on now".

Sharing the control with children may be quite challenging for some parents, as this isn't something that everybody feels comfortable with. However, it's important to realise that offering Limited Choices allows you to share control on your terms instead of letting your child take over. Sharing the control in this way also helps to fulfil a child's need for Freedom and Autonomy, Power and Significance and for Belonging. It shows children that we are prepared to trust them, helps to give them a sense of control over the situation and shows them that their opinion matters and that their feelings are being heard.

This will also make them far less resistant to the occasional need to make an executive or emergency decision on their behalf. In other words, provided that they realise that they are allowed to choose for themselves most of the time, they will be less likely to argue with us when we are forced by circumstance to issue an order.

Finally, choices also allow children to practice making decisions (good and bad) early on, so it's the best preparation for the 'real world'.

How to use Limited Choices:

1. When faced with a situation where you want a child to do something, think of two limited choices or options that suit you.

2. Present these choices before your child has a chance to oppose what you might suggest (i.e. before a power struggle occurs).

3. Ask your child to choose between the two options. For example in Jack and Chloe's scenario above:

   a) "Do you want to stop playing now or in five minutes?", which is much more effective than "You need to stop playing in five minutes" (although this is still better than 'Tidy up your toys immediately').

   b) "Would you like to wash your hands first or tidy up first?" Only offer these choices if you are happy with the outcome of both, as you might consider that washing hands must absolutely come after tidying up.

   c) "Would you like to tidy up your toys now or after dinner?", if this is a choice that you can live with.

4. You should avoid using disguised threats or rewards within your choices such as "Would you rather continue what you're doing or not watch TV tonight?". Even though this is asked as a question, this is not offering your child any choice and is actually a threat in disguise!

5. If your child chooses a third option, not offered (some children will do this every time!), simply ask them, "What were the choices I gave you?", and ask them once again to choose between your options rather than their own.

6. If they don't make a choice within a reasonable amount of time, or say "No", then you choose for them. As they won't be happy,

and they might have an outburst, tell them with empathy: "You will get more choices later".

7. Give Limited Choices as often as possible because the more control you give, the more you get back: by making enough 'deposits', you can make 'withdrawals'. So giving enough choices each day will make your child much more compliant when you have to give an order, especially if you accompany this order with something along the lines of: "I usually give choices, but not this time".

NB: Some parents' reaction to this technique is that it would take too long to give so many choices. But the reality is that with a bit of practice, these choices start to come naturally and will save you a lot of time that might be currently wasted in opposition, power struggles and arguing and negotiation. The majority of parents who implement this tool report saving up to one hour a day just by using it consistently.

Further examples for solving typical parenting challenges

1. Child refusing to cooperate

You could ask your child "Do you want to brush your teeth now or in a couple of minutes?"

2. Child not listening/Ignoring you

"Would you rather tidy your room now, or after you've finished your drawing?"

3. Child arguing and negotiating

"Would you rather keep arguing about this or play this game with me instead?"

4. Child refusing or making a fuss over homework

"Would you like to do your homework now or after you had a snack?"
Or, "Would you like to do your homework sitting beside me or up in your own room?"

✖ TOOL #7
Asking Questions

Objective: Encouraging children to think for themselves and making them more responsive to our requests

"Judge a man by his questions rather than his answers."
Voltaire, Philosopher,
Historian & French Enlightenment writer

"My greatest strength as a consultant is to be
ignorant and ask a few questions."
Peter Drucker, Management Consultant,
Author & Business Visionary

Effective leaders realise the importance of empowering their teams, and refrain from hovering over individual team members to remind them what they should be doing. Instead, leaders will clarify expectations and use more subtle ways to ensure their teams do what they are supposed to do.

We often find ourselves nagging our children and reminding them to do things that they already know they should be doing. This is an exhausting and ineffectual task for the parent. When we constantly remind our children to do things, they will often start ignoring us because they get used to us giving them a number of reminders before we actually do something about it (such as raising our voice or getting angry).

Mollie walks through her front door after a particularly stressful day at work; she goes to the kitchen, switches on the kettle and hears the children arriving back from school:

"How was school?" She asks.

"It was okay." James (5) replies, as he drops his school bag on the kitchen floor.

"Pick your school bag up and put it away where it belongs, James. Dinner will be in half an hour so make sure you wash your hands before you eat and don't forget that you also have homework to do. What about you Sasha (8), how was your day?"

"It was fine."

"You have swimming practice later on. Don't forget to pack your swimming goggles this time! If you have homework to do you better get a move on because we need to be out of the house no later than 6 O'clock. Are you even listening to me, Sasha?!"

How to become a Leader parent

Mollie would have found getting her children to do what they need to do much easier if she'd engaged them into 'thinking mode' by asking them questions – other than 'how was school today?'.

When children are in thinking mode, this makes them less likely to be confrontational and more inclined to listen to us and to be more cooperative and compliant to our requests. Asking children questions instead of using nagging and reminding also encourages them to think about their actions and question their own behaviour, which better equips them to be self-disciplined and responsible in adult life.

How to use Asking Questions:

If you've made your expectations clear and have already told a child a few times that they are supposed to do something, instead of reminding them or correcting them, you can use this tool in the following circumstances:

1. For Routines:

In the scenario described above, Mollie could use a series of questions:

"What are you supposed to do with your school bag?" or "What do we do when we come back from school?"

"What do we do before eating?"

"Do you have anything to prepare for school tomorrow?"

"Do you remember what activity you have later on?"

"What do you need to put in your bag to go swimming?"

2. **To develop good habits:**

   "What do we say when we receive a gift?" instead of "Say thank you".

3. **When children are not behaving appropriately:**

   If your child is misbehaving (for example, they have invited a friend over and they are not following the house rules), simply ask, **"How do we do this in this house?"**

4. **When children are asking you for something that they know they can't have:**

   If your child asks you: "Can I have an ice cream" when it's 30 minutes until dinner, try responding with another question: **"What do you think?"** or if they tend to answer "Yes", **"What time do we have an ice cream or sweets?"**.

5. **When children make a mistake:**

   If a child needs to be corrected (for example, if they spill a drink), rather than resorting to blame and nagging simply ask: **"What could you do about this?"**

   More often than not, they will already know how to deal with the situation and will clean up the mess. Your job as a parent is to encourage them to reach this point by engaging their attention and getting them to think for themselves.

   When children are still a little confused or unsure as to what to do next, they may benefit from a bit of coaching, so try asking them, "Do you want some ideas as to what you could do about this situation?" - then give them ideas of what they could do using **Limited Choices** (Tool #6).

6. **You can also use Asking Questions to help your children open up and share:**

   In Mollie's example above, asking her children "How was school today?" received a typical answer of 'Ok'. There are much more effective questions that you can ask your children to help them open up:

- "What was your best moment at school today? (Or what was your worst moment at school today?)

- What did you learn today?

- When were you happiest today?

- What part of the day do you look forward to? What part of the day do you dread?

- Who did you help today? Who helped you today?

- What are you grateful for today?

Once they start speaking, it's essential that you allow them to speak freely and that you refrain from judgement. If they share something that's bothering them, resist the urge to intervene and try to fix things for them. Instead, use **Emotion Coaching** (Tool #17). This will make them want to share even more in future.

❌ TOOL #8
Positive & Enforceable Statements

Objective: Replacing fear and threats with a positive alternative to prevent power struggles and increase cooperation

'*Empty threats are often worse than saying nothing at all. It's like leading from behind. Eventually, no one thinks you're leading at all. And after a while, no one is even listening.*'
Kathleen Troia McFarland, Former Deputy Assistant Secretary of Defence for Public Affairs

Leading out of fear and using threats may be effective to get people to do things in the short-term, but it often backfires because it creates resentment and doesn't motivate people to want to do their best. Successful leaders find more positive ways to get their team to do what has to be done by communicating in a way that does not alienate or demotivate their team members.

We often resort to using fear and threats in order to try to get our children to do as they are supposed to, especially when we are feeling stressed, tired or overworked. The problem is that such threats and fear tactics usually end up falling on 'deaf' and defiant ears, and can cause our children to become resistant and even less likely to comply with our requests.

Moreover, children will try to test our resolve, as 'testing the limits' is part of growing up and learning what works and what doesn't. And if they realise that we are not following through on the statement we have made and that our threat was actually an empty one, they are even more likely to start ignoring our threats, until we up the ante. This inevitably becomes a vicious circle of more empty threats and only serves to undermine our authority further over time.

Anna sits down at dinner table to eat an evening meal with the family:

"What's the matter Kirstie (8), I thought you liked pasta?" Anna asks, as Kirstie uses her fork to push the food around his plate.

"I did, but I wanted pizza tonight."

"Well, I've made pasta, so eat it up before it gets cold – we can have pizza another night."

"But that's not fair!"

"Kirstie, would you please just eat your dinner!"

"But I don't want it!"

"Fine, if you don't eat what I've just spent the last hour preparing for you, then you won't have dessert.

And as Kirstie is still not eating, Anna ups the ante: "And if you won't eat, you can forget about me taking you to the theme park this weekend!"

Kirstie barely touches her food and doesn't speak another word for the rest of the meal. In the back of her mind, she's hoping that her Mum won't follow through with her threat as she often doesn't.

Wouldn't it be great to avoid this sort of common scenario by having an alternative to threats that doesn't create as much resistance from children, and also makes it more likely that we actually follow through on our word?

How to become a Leader parent

This tool is called Positive & Enforceable Statements because it is all about being able to enforce whatever we say; it highlights the importance of focusing on what we can 'control' rather than focusing on the things that we have no control over.

How to use Enforceable Statements:

1. It's important that your statement addresses something that you can control and enforce.

2. **Start your statement with:**

    a) **'I'** (or 'We' if we are speaking about both parents). For example: Kirstie would have responded more positively if Anna had said, "I give dessert to children who have finished their meal" or "I take children to the theme park who eat what I cook for them" (although this is unrelated and therefore not generally advisable).

    Note the use of the third person 'children', which will make this more effective, particularly for parents with more than one child.

    b) **"Children who…'**, for example: "Children who want to go to the park must have put away their toys."

    c) **"You can do … as soon as …"**, for example: "You can play with your friends as soon as you've helped me put the shopping away."

3. **Keep the sentence positive**: you are making a statement of fact rather than a threat.

4. **Follow through and do not give in**. For these statements to really be effective, ensure that you enforce them as otherwise you undermine your own authority, and children will be even less likely to take your word seriously in future. Perseverance is key: children may initially try to argue, but will soon learn from experience that you mean what you say and when faced with a Positive & Enforceable Statement they'll realise there is no point in putting up a fight.

NB: It is very easy to slip back into making threats while still believing you are making an Enforceable Statement. For example, "I take children to the park who have tidied their room", can easily become "I won't take you to the park until you've tidied your room." These two sentences are very similar, but the key difference is that the first statement is far more effective because it focuses on the positive rather than the conditional, and doesn't address the child directly. It is therefore much less likely to be taken personally by a child, unlike a threat.

Further examples for solving typical parenting challenges

1. Child not listening/Ignoring you

"I listen to children who listen to me."

2. Child refusing or making a fuss over homework

"I am happy to take you to your friend's house as soon as you have finished your homework."
Or, "I give ideas to children who have already started their homework."

3. Whining

"I listen to children who speak in the same tone of voice as mine."

4. Morning Issues: Taking too long to do everything

"My car leaves in five minutes and I take children to school dressed or not dressed." This works better if you take children to school by car as you need to follow through. If they are not dressed on time, you should take the remaining clothes in a bag: they will usually get dressed in the car before arriving at school. This may sound a bit harsh but if you manage to follow-through, they are much more likely to get dressed on time the next day!

✖ TOOL #9
Positive Redirection

Objective: *Increasing positive interactions at home in order to prevent power struggles and tantrums, making children more cooperative*

> *"If we understood the awesome power of our words, we would prefer silence to almost anything negative."*
> **Betty Eadie, Author of NYT Best-Seller 'Embraced by Light'**

Good leaders recognise that positive statements are much more effective than negative ones when encouraging team members to cooperate with their superiors as well as with one another. They will therefore avoid using negative statements unless they are left with no other choice.

Some research states that as much as 80% of our interaction with our children is in the form of negative statements such as 'No you can't have ice cream before dinner,' or 'Stop slamming that door!'. Of course, we have to tell children 'No' occasionally, but the problem is that if we say it too often, it starts to lose its effectiveness. The other issue is when we use too many negative statements, this puts children into 'opposition mode'. When they are in opposition mode, they become uncooperative and resistant, which increases the likelihood that they will start to use the word 'No' themselves indiscriminately.

It's almost dinnertime, when Chloe (6) walks into the kitchen and asks Jack: "Dad, can I have some crisps?"

"Are you kidding me? You know that dinner is ready in five minutes so the answer is obviously no!"

"But Dad, that's not fair! I'm hungry right now!"

"Chloe, you know perfectly well that this isn't the right time, now go and wash your hands and stop bothering me with silly questions."

Chloe stomps off as Peter (14) walks into the room and asks: "Where's the charger for the iPad?"

"No, you can forget it. You're not playing on that iPad until you've finished your homework."

"I wasn't going to play, I need it for my homework research" Peter says and he continues looking for the iPad charger.

How to become a Leader parent

Children are innately curious, and some of them are born explorers, therefore it is perfectly normal for them to test the limits and misbehave from time to time. But if we can replace even half of the negative statements that we use towards our children with a more positive alternative, then on those occasions when we do have to say 'No', they will be far more likely to comply.

As psychologists have found, putting a positive spin to short commands such as 'No' (rather than focusing on the behaviour that we want our children to stop, for example, "Stop yelling,") is much more effective[21]. It's also worth remembering that some kids will keep repeating the same misguided behaviour, simply because they don't know how else it should be done. It's easy to forget that just as kids don't come with a manual, neither do they come with instructions for how to behave. It is therefore essential to express our expectations clearly and positively.

When and how to use Positive Redirection:

I. **If your child is asking for something that you're not willing to give them:**

1. You should try to always begin your answer with a 'Yes' regardless of whether you intend to grant the request or not.

2. This allows you to redirect their request. For example:

- In Jack's case, rather than answering Chloe's request for crisps with an emphatic 'No', it's better to say: "Yes, you can have crisps tomorrow at snack time."

- As an answer to "I want this toy", use "Yes, you can put this on your birthday list", rather than: "There's no way I'm buying you this now!".

- As an answer to "Can I have a pony?" try "Sure, you can have a pony when you're old enough and rich enough to buy one", instead of: "No, you can't have a pony, what are you thinking?!".

NB: Parents are often surprised by how often children are willing to be reasonable – they are more than capable of realising for themselves when it's not the right moment!

II. **If your child is doing something that you want them to stop doing:**

1. Use a positive command (also called a 'start command') expressed firmly and ideally without raising your voice (see example below).

2. If possible, suggest an alternative activity or an alternative way of doing things.

   Examples:

- "Please speak quietly" - instead of: "Stop Yelling."

- "Gently pet the dog" - instead of: "Stop hurting the dog."

- "Please close the door gently, would you like me to show you how?" - instead of: "Don't slam the door!"

- "Hang on tight" - instead of: "Careful you might fall."

Further examples for solving typical parenting challenges

1. Tantrums

"Sure, you can have this sweet after lunch." Instead of: "No! You can't have this sweet as you haven't had lunch yet".

2. Arguing and Negotiating

"Sure we can go to the park once you have finished your homework" instead of "No you can't go to the park, and you know perfectly well why: you still haven't done your homework!"

3. Child feeling insecure or lacking confidence

Try to limit the amount of times that you use the word 'No' and replace it with more positive sentences. See **Growth Mindset - Tool #20.**

❌ TOOL #10
Effective Communication

Objective: *Ensuring children listen to us while keeping the connection with them.*

"The art of communication is the language of leadership."
James Humes, Author of
'Speak Like Churchill, Stand Like Lincoln'

"In many ways, effective communication begins
with mutual respect, communication that inspires,
encourages others to do their best."
Zig Ziglar, Author of 'See You at the Top'

Strong communication skills are essential in the corporate world; being able to communicate confidently and effectively helps to ensure that each member of the team is working together towards the same goal.

We often bark orders at our children without even being aware of it, particularly when they are at a distance. When we are tired or in a hurry, we are far more likely to react to our children's misbehaviour with a sense of annoyance and impatience. So instead of sitting down with our children and speaking to them properly, we shout orders from across the park or from the other side of the supermarket, "Stop doing that!" or "No more chasing your sister!". We raise our voice, either because we want to ensure that we are actually heard, because we want quick obedience, or because we are getting angry at them for not complying with our orders. But this is seldom effective and our children learn to ignore us.

Children respond far better to calm and focused communication in the same way adults do. As explained in **Understanding Your Children** (Tool #3), when they are yelled at, even if anger is not our intention, it makes them more likely to 'shut down' and refuse to listen to us whatsoever. This physiological reaction makes it almost impossible for them to 'hear' what we are saying.

Worse still, shouting doesn't teach them how to regulate and be in control of their own emotions, because we aren't modelling this behaviour ourselves (see Tool #12 - **Leading by Example**).

Mollie is preparing dinner and shouts from the kitchen: "Sasha (8), turn that tablet off and come and set the table!"

She gets no answer: "Sasha, did you hear what I said? I need you to come and set the table now!" She still doesn't get a reply, so she marches into the living room and shouts right into Sasha's face:

"What is the matter with you – I've asked you twice now to lay the table, can you not hear me?! Don't make me ask you a third time, or I swear that I'll ground you."

Sasha suddenly freezes, her eyes widen and she doesn't seem to be listening to Mollie at all.

"Right, I've had enough of this – I'll just go and lay the table myself."

She goes back to the kitchen leaving Sasha, standing still and silent with a very sad look on her face.

How to become a Leader parent

There are several key things that we can do to make our communication with our children more effective.

For example, as we saw earlier, communication is improved and conflict reduced when we allow children to stop what they are doing by offering a limited choice. This helps children who can find it incredibly difficult to break their focus and simply 'switch' to something else. This is particularly true of younger children, who may become so absorbed in an activity that they find it very difficult to be aware of much else.

How to use Effective Communication:

1. **Control your reactions using ABC:** It's essential to become aware of your physiological response to your child's behaviour and to try to stop yourself before the frustration or anger takes over. A good way to do this is to acknowledge the emotions

that you are experiencing as this helps to diffuse them. So once you feel yourself 'triggered', it's useful to take a few deep breaths, and then remind yourself that you have a choice about how you are going to react.

This choice determines whether your child 'shuts down', as Sasha does in the scenario above, or is motivated to do what you are asking of them. A good trick to remember these 3 steps is to use the acronym ABC: A = Acknowledge your feelings, B = Breathe deeply and C = Choice and Control over your reactions.

2. **Speak to children when you're close to them**: Try not to call out from a distance, unless in an emergency. Instead, it's much better to move closer to them, get down to their level, try to make eye contact with them (but be aware that they may not be ready for this so don't force it), and speak to them softly. Or even better whisper, as children usually react very positively to this.

3. **Allow some time for them to do what you ask**: Try as much as possible to leave a bit of time for the child to finish what they are doing or to carry out your requests. A good tactic is to ask them whether they want to do what you've asked now or in five minutes (See Tool #6 - **Limited Choices**).

4. **Try not to use many reminders and nagging**. To keep check of this, when talking to your children, ask yourself: "Is this new information that I am giving?" If it isn't (and this is often the case!), then use the tool **Asking Questions** (#7).

5. **Avoid doing too much explaining**, particularly when there is tension in the air. The more words you use, the less effective you become.

6. **Do not 'box' them or label them**: Labelling your child 'naughty', 'bad boy/girl', 'the challenging one', 'over-sensitive', 'cry baby', etc. can backfire as it can lead to them adopting this identity. We need to allow children to develop their own identity, rather than 'boxing' them into one, particularly in the early years. Even using more positive labels such as 'good' or 'smart' is a judgement and can be detrimental in the long-term

as children can become afraid of 'losing' this label (See Tool # 20 - **Growth Mindset**).

7. **Do not compare them to others**: You should take care to never compare your kids to other friends or to their siblings - even if it's very tempting to make an example of one child who is doing just what we've asked, to try to improve the behaviour of another child who is being more challenging.

⊗ TOOL #11
Setting Rules & Clarifying Expectations

Objective: *Establishing boundaries and foundations for family life*

*"As a leader, you are always going to get a combination
of two things: What you create and What you allow."*
**Henry Cloud, Clinical psychologist,
Leadership Expert & Best-Selling Author**

Rules and clear expectations give staff a sense of stability and a framework within which they can express their autonomy. These rules and expectations therefore help a business to run more efficiently.

Whether we happen to be in a corporate setting or at home with our family, if those around us don't have a very clear understanding of the rules and what is expected of them, it makes it much more difficult for them to know how to behave.

'Be good' or 'Behave' are probably the phrases we use most commonly with our children, but this is quite vague for a child and we may not have first made our expectations of what it means to 'behave' and 'be good' very clear - which can be a tall order!

There are clear rules in the corporate world and at school, so it's perfectly reasonable that there should also be rules in the household. Setting clear household rules also has the advantage of teaching children that rules, whether they happen to be household rules, school rules or otherwise, are to be complied with.

Chloe (6) is playing in the living room with her toys scattered on the floor:

"Mummy, I'm tired of playing with these toys, I want to do some colouring in now."

"Okay Chloe (6), I'll get your colouring book for you as soon as you tidy away your toys."

"But Mummy, I want to do colouring in now. I'll put my toys away later."

"Chloe, you know our house rule, if you want to play with something else you have to put your other toys away first."

Tears fill Chloe's eyes:

"Okay, I suppose we can make an exception. I'll go and get your colouring book as long as you promise to pick your toys up later on."

Evening arrives and Jack comes in from work to find Chloe's toys still scattered across the living room floor.

How to become a Leader parent

Children need boundaries, particularly when they are younger, to provide them with a sense of stability and security. The clearer the expectations the better, as it is this sense of certainty that helps them to understand what is and isn't acceptable.

However, children also need expectations to be specific and made clear as they cannot comply with hundreds of rules, and they cannot be expected to know what it means to 'behave' or 'be good' in all circumstances.

These boundaries set a framework for the child's behaviour and their objective isn't to stifle them. Quite the contrary, these boundaries create a framework within which the parent will need to give their child the autonomy to make mistakes and to learn from them (see Tool #18 - **Mistakes as Opportunities for Learning**).

As our children grow older (six upwards), we can start involving them in setting house rules. Although the parents are the ultimate decision makers, it is important that children are allowed to express an opinion and have their thoughts and feelings heard. This is best done in the setting of a **Family Meeting** (see Tool #22).

The key to setting household rules and clarifying expectations is to do so in a way that encourages cooperation rather than power struggles. We can do this by setting rules in a loving and non-confrontational way.

How to set rules and clarify expectations:

1. **Define some household rules with your partner**. Define what is acceptable and what is unacceptable (refer to Tool #2 - **Teamwork**).

2. **KISS - Keep it short and simple** - if the household rules are short and simple, this increases the likelihood that they will be remembered and adhered to.

3. **Avoid using disguised threats**.

4. **Express your loving limit in the third person** - even if you only have one child - and as positively as possible. For example try, "In this house, children who want to eat must remain seated at the table", rather than, "If you don't sit still at the table, I'm taking your plate away and they'll be no more dinner for you".
   Or, "Children don't hit their siblings in this house", instead of "If you keep hitting your sister like that, you're going to go to your room!". Although this statement isn't a positive one, the use of the third person makes it much less confrontational and the effect on children is far more effective as a result.

5. **Try to avoid negative statements** such as "You can't…" or "You're not allowed to…". Instead, try to replace it with a cheerier, more positive alternative.

6. When setting a new rule, make sure that this is clear to everyone by stating "The new rule in this house is…".

7. To make sure that everyone understands the new rule, ask your children to repeat it back to you.

NB: Remember that when it comes to parenting, actions speak louder than words! So on the occasions when children disobey us by breaking a household rule that the family has previously agreed on, we should try to keep our words to a minimum and ensure that we follow through with a Logical Consequence (see Tool #19 - **Logical and Delayed Consequences**). Being consistent is especially important when introducing a new rule or expectation as it shows children that we are serious and mean what we say. If like Anna, we set a rule but aren't consistent in enforcing it, our children are likely not to trust our word in future.

Further examples for solving typical parenting challenges

1. Child refusing to cooperate

"This is the new rule: in this house, children have to tidy their room by the end of each day."

2. Child not listening/Ignoring you

"This is the new rule: in this house, we do things for children who listen to us."

3. Whining

"In this family, children who whine don't get what they are asking for."

4. Child refusing or making a fuss over homework

"In this family, we complete our work before we play."

5. Child hooked on screens, TV, iPads and other electronic devices

"In this house, children can only use screens for half an hour a day" - or whatever works for your household and your child's age.

How to Communicate Effectively to Meet Children's Needs

- The more control we give, the more we get back: offering children Limited Choices gives them an opportunity to practice making decisions and fulfils their basic need for autonomy and control.

- It's important to take care to never use disguised threats or rewards within our choices.

- Engaging children into 'thinking mode' rather than 'opposition mode' by Asking Questions encourages them to be more cooperative and compliant to requests.

- Replace nagging and reminding with Asking Questions - this encourages kids to think about their actions and question their own behaviour, which increases the likelihood of them growing to become responsible and self-disciplined adults.

- Focus on what you can 'control' rather than focusing on the things that you have no control over and eliminate empty threats.

- When we make a Positive & Enforceable Statement, we need to make sure that it is stated positively and that we follow through and do not give in as this will only serve to undermine our authority.

- Avoid using the word 'No' wherever possible because if we use this word too often it will lose its effectiveness over time.

- Replace negative statements such as "No you can't..." or "Stop doing that!" with a more positive alternative as this will make children more likely to want to comply with your requests.

- Try to avoid resorting to shouting or yelling at children - this is seldom effective and children learn to ignore you.

- Children respond far better to calm and focused communication in the exact same way adults do so we should speak to them as we would wish to be spoken to.

- Implement clear rules and set boundaries by making your expectations clear to provide children with a sense of stability and security.

- The key to setting and enforcing household rules is to do so in a way that encourages cooperation rather than power struggles - do this by implementing rules in a non-confrontational way, using the third person and phrasing the statement in a positive way.

Your Notes

CHAPTER 4

Leading by Example, Motivating & Inspiring

In corporate life, the most successful leaders are those who lead by example and who motivate and inspire their colleagues and team members. Yet in family life, we sometimes fall short of applying these same principles.

We may need to go to a meeting and our kids are taking ages to get ready, or we've had a long and demanding day at work and they start 'mis'behaving because they are craving our time and attention. It is in moments like these, when we are feeling stressed and overwhelmed that it's easy to find ourselves being triggered.

Because of the stress and rush, we may resort to shouting at our children in an attempt to regain control of the situation. But instead of calming things down, as we saw earlier, shouting often increases stress levels and only makes matters worse.

Other days, we might find ourselves giving in to our children's whining and arguing to avoid getting into a power struggle with them. This is often exacerbated by feelings of guilt about having such little time to spend with them. When we are inconsistent in this way, we reinforce our children's belief that whining and arguing can get them what they want, and therefore increase the likelihood of experiencing power struggles with our children in the future.

It can also be difficult to find the time to take good care of ourselves when we're busy trying to juggle work and family life. So it's not unusual for working parents to find that they start to neglect their own needs, which sets a bad example for children. More on this in **Taking Good Care of Yourself** (Tool #13).

As with our colleagues or team members, respect, motivation and inspiration are fundamental to bolstering the relationship we have with our children. Therefore, learning to become more patient and consistent in our approach is key to successful parenting. In order to help us achieve this, we have adapted some of the key workplace skills to help parents:

- Lead by example at home.
- Define family values that will give a sense of purpose to your family members.
- Learn to take better care of yourself so you can take better care of your family.

✖ TOOL #12
Leading by Example

Objective: Inspiring children through action rather than words and being the best role model that we can be

"The three most important ways to lead people are:...
by example... by example... by example."
Albert Schweitzer, Theologian, Philosopher & Physician

"If your actions create a legacy that inspires others to dream more,
learn more, do more and become more, then,
you are an excellent leader."
Dolly Parton, singer, actress, author and businesswoman

Leading by example is at the pinnacle of good leadership, as it is the best way to gain respect and motivate colleagues and fellow team members towards success. Through their actions rather than words, a leader uplifts, encourages and inspires those around them to 'give it their all' and fulfil their potential.

In our family lives, we often expect children to 'do as we say, not as we do', instead of leading by example and modelling the behaviour we wish to see, as we would naturally do in the workplace. Respect breeds respect, so if we wish for our children to treat us with respect and be motivated to do their best, the most effective way to achieve this is to first adopt such values ourselves and strive to model them in our own lives.

That said, leading by example is often far easier said than done, especially during moments when we are feeling stressed or overwhelmed. In these situations, it can be incredibly difficult to keep emotions in check and stop them from clouding our judgement and affecting our behaviour.

Jack is reading a newspaper in the living room, while his daughter, Kirstie (8), watches TV:

"Kirstie, I've already asked you once to turn the TV down. Don't make me ask you a second time."

Kirstie is so enthralled by what she is watching and doesn't even turn to look at Jack.

"Don't ignore me when I'm talking to you! Now do as you are told, I can't hear myself think with all that noise!" Jack shouts at twice the volume of the TV.

Later that evening, they are eating dinner, and Kirstie is refusing to finish her dinner:

"You need to eat the rest of your veggies, Kirstie. Now stop being silly and do as you're told."

"Why should I? I don't even like carrots, you can't make me eat them!?" Kirstie shouts at her father, before pushing her dinner plate half way across the kitchen table.

"How dare you shout at me – I will not tolerate shouting in this house! If you don't want to eat your dinner, then you can just go to your room instead!" Jack shouts back, as Kirstie stomps off with her arms crossed and a frown on her face.

As parents, it's important that we try to find more constructive ways to cope than shouting or losing our temper, because otherwise we risk setting a very poor example for our kids who look to us for support and guidance.

To be an inspiring model to our children - and it may sound like a tall order - we should show them that we are self-aware, in control of our own emotions and able to approach life's challenges with confidence. By setting a good example of leadership in this way, we are teaching our children to adopt the same values and characteristics.

How to become a Leader parent

Leading by example is a powerful way to achieve long-lasting positive change in family life because it inspires children through actions rather than words alone.

Indeed, leading by example is also about recognising and being proud of being a role model as a working parent, rather that feeling guilty about it. Research shows that daughters of working mothers are more likely to be successful later in life because their mothers provided a good role model for them[22].

We need to recognise the benefits that we provide for our children when we pursue our dreams and live a satisfied life, whether that means working a job we love or staying at home to raise our kids. We provide a service to our children by being a role model who has a fulfilled life; in this way we teach them that life is about balancing priorities and give and take.

That said, we need to take care to avoid the 'perfect' parent trap, as it would take a superhuman to achieve all of the 'leading by example items' listed below. We need to accept that we are only human and as a result, are prone to making mistakes now and then. This is another very important aspect of leading by example as it's important to model the fact that we can take responsibility for our actions and our mistakes (more on this in Tool #18 - **Mistakes as Opportunities for Learning**).

The first step is to try to be more aware of what we are saying and how we are saying it, and to recognise that challenging moments can be an invaluable teaching opportunity, both at home and in the workplace. When we strive to deal with such moments in a constructive way, we demonstrate through our own speech and actions how our children can cope when they are faced with similar challenges. Equally, by modelling the behaviours we would like to see in our children, such as respect, kindness and empathy, we teach them to internalise these values and display these attributes in their own lives.

How to Lead by Example in your family life:

1. Always show respect for yourself, other people and the environment. Although it is sometimes difficult to be respectful to our children when we are in a hurry or when they 'push our buttons', be aware that they learn from us so we can only hold them to the same standards we set ourselves.

2. If you feel guilty for not seeing your child enough or if they use 'emotional blackmail' to make you feel guilty, remember that by working, you are being a good role model. Tell your children that you love them and that you always try to put them first, but that this isn't always possible. Explain why your job is also important and you therefore have to balance priorities.

3. Learn to regulate your own emotions so that your children can learn to control theirs. If, like Jack, you have a tendency to shout/yell, it's important that you try to find alternative ways of reacting to stressful situations. See Tool #10 - **Effective Communication** for examples of ways to respond to stressful situations more effectively.

4. Model patience and the delaying of gratification. Parenting probably requires more patience than any other job and it's very difficult to be patient when children trigger us, but it's much more difficult for children to learn to be patient and delay gratification if parents don't first model this themselves.

5. Take good care of yourself by ensuring that as many as possible of your mental, physical and emotional needs are met because otherwise, you're sending the message that it's okay to disregard personal needs and the danger is that children will tend to model the same behaviour. See Tool #13 - **Taking Good Care of Yourself**.

6. Emotions and feelings are contagious (see mirror neurons in Tool #3 - **Understanding Your Children**). Therefore, it's better to always try to be as positive and joyful as possible (which can be difficult after a stressful day at work), and be mindful of your 'self-talk', which will influence children. This is particularly important if you feel that your children are going through a 'negativity phase'.

7. If you wish for your children to be kind, well-mannered and empathetic, ensure that you act in this way in your dealings with people.

8. If you want them to have good table manners, one of the most important actions is to have meals together as often as possible - and to obviously model good table manners when you do! This is particularly tough for working parents, but research shows that spending more mealtimes together as a family is the biggest predictor of good manners as well as good behaviour.

9. Model sharing and gratitude: at the end of each day, either during dinner or at bedtime, express gratitude for some of the things that have happened that day. And then ask them to share their happiest moments for which they are grateful. As children grow older, you could add to this 'ritual' the sharing of mistakes made during the day and initiate a discussion about what can be learnt from those mistakes (see Tool #19 – **Mistakes as Opportunities for Learning**).

Further examples for solving typical parenting challenges

1. Child hooked on screens, TV, iPads and other electronic devices

Restricting your own screen time and trying not to check your phone constantly in front of your kids is a great example that you can set for your children. You could also introduce a rule such as 'no screens at mealtime' that would apply to all members of the family.

2. Child back-chatting, being rude and swearing at you or other people

Check in with yourself as to whether your children are copying your behaviour, and make sure that you don't use 'rude' words in front of them or with others.

3. Child being bossy

It is natural for your child to reproduce what they see and hear. Be aware of this and try to reduce your own 'bossiness' (see **Chapter 2** for alternatives to orders/commands and nagging).

✹ TOOL #13
Taking Good Care of Yourself

Objective: Restoring your energy levels and putting things into perspective

---

"You best teach others about healthy boundaries by enforcing yours."
Bryant McGill, Author of 'Simple Reminders:
Inspiration for Living Your Best Life'

"It's not selfish to love yourself, take care of yourself,
and to make your happiness a priority. It's necessary."
Mandy Hale, Author of 'The Single Woman:
Life, Love & a Dash of Sass'

Effective leaders recognise the importance of work-life harmony and that taking good care of their own health and emotional wellbeing has a 'drip-down' effect on the rest of the team, in that it inspires others to take equal care of themselves. And by taking good care of themselves they are then better placed to take care of the needs of others.

Most parents lead very busy lives, particularly if both parents are working, so it's quite common to put some of our own needs aside in our everyday life. Also, because we are likely not to spend as much time with our children as we'd like, it can be all too easy to get caught in a cycle of guilt and self-recrimination. So we may find ourselves overcompensating for this by often putting our children's needs ahead of our own, even if it means that our own needs go unmet in the process.

The issue is that if we do this for a long period of time, our work-life harmony is affected and it is likely to influence us negatively, and subsequently our relationship with the rest of the family. Indeed, in order to take good care of others, we must first take good care of ourselves by prioritising our own needs.

Similarly, when we are stressed at work, we may bring this stress home without realising it and get 'triggered' by our children more easily than usual, which can also have a negative impact on the family dynamic.

Anna and her family are in the living room on a Sunday afternoon. Jack and Anna are talking, while the kids play with their toys:

"Jack, I'm really worried about all the new changes they've been making at work recently – I'm not even clear what my role is anymore."

"You probably only feel like that because you're so exhausted right now, things will look better after a good night's…"

Jack is interrupted by the sound of Chloe (6) spilling the contents of a board game all over the floor. Counters and dice scatter everywhere, which the kids find funny so they start giggling:

"What on earth is the matter with you?! Can't you just play quietly for once without making a mess everywhere?" Anna snaps.

The children freeze and look at each other in confusion as Anna is usually so patient and understanding with them. Jack is almost as surprised by Anna's reaction as the children are, so he quietly ushers them into the kitchen for a snack leaving a now guilty-looking Anna to compose herself.

How to become a Leader parent

An awareness of our needs and what makes us happy is essential to be able to prioritise and achieve better work-life harmony. Also, an awareness of our limitations and 'shortcomings' as a parent can be constructive as it helps us to identify which aspects of our parenting we would like to change or improve upon.

It's only natural that we want to be the best parent to our children that we can, so we may find ourselves trying to 'measure up' to an idealised notion of the 'perfect parent' and then feel a failure when we don't live up to that expectation.

To avoid falling into these common parenting traps, we need to recognise when they arise and be more forgiving (of ourselves, our children and our partner), focus on taking good care of ourselves and ensuring our own needs are being met. This will help to restore our energy, revitalises our sense of self and reduces stress levels.

Living a fulfilling life by showing that a balance can be achieved between work, rest and play provides an important service to our children in that we are providing them with a role model. Indeed, the impact of endeavouring to take better care of ourselves is both profound and far-reaching because when we thrive, so do the rest of our family. Our happiness and enthusiasm helps to motivate and inspire our children and when we take care of ourselves, they will also learn to do the same for themselves, which makes it a win-win situation.

How to take good care of yourself:

Look at Glasser's five key human needs (see Tool #3 – **Understanding our Children**) and evaluate whether you are addressing these needs in your own life. Create an action plan to better address these needs, using some of the ideas below:

- Give yourself some 'me time'. We can become so consumed in our role as parents that we end up exhausting ourselves by trying to attend to everyone else's needs, and in the process forget to take care of our own. Remember, acting the martyr doesn't do you or your children any favours, as not only will you be a poor role model, but you will also miss out on the most pleasurable aspects of parenting.

- Identify which activities you enjoy most and that are likely to help you relax and 'recharge your batteries' (e.g. sports, museums, eating out, etc.) and try to schedule in this 'me' time every week. If you aren't able to schedule in this time for whatever reason, then involve your children in some of your hobbies; parents are often pleasantly surprised to find that their children enjoy activities such as gardening, walking etc. just as much as they do.

- Be kind to yourself, allow yourself room to make mistakes, and avoid falling into common parenting traps such as the 'perfect parent' or blaming yourself or your children when things go wrong. It is okay to cut corners at times.

- When you feel yourself getting angry, rather than letting it get to a point where you start shouting, step back from the situation by taking a deep breath and continue breathing deeply while being conscious of your emotions. This will help to relieve any negative emotions that you may be experiencing (such as frustration), enabling you to respond in a more balanced and effective way.

- Remember that no matter what the situation, you have the choice to respond in a more constructive way, and it is sometimes better not to address the situation immediately if you are triggered (see Tool #19 - **Logical and Delayed Consequences**).

- One of the most rewarding things to do is to take the time to enjoy your children one-on-one (see **Presence** - Tool #16), separate from usual obligations. This allows you to connect with them through laughter and play and meet your need for Love and Belonging in the process.

- Reach out to other parents. It's amazing how many parents feel alone with a problem and suffer in silence only to find that other parents are facing exactly the same challenges.

- It's essential that you ask for help when you need it and that you are also 'taken care of'. We often expect others to instinctively know that we have too much on our plate and that we need help, but it's much better to express ourselves before we become so overwhelmed that our negative emotions take over. This also means being able to delegate and trust others to do a 'good enough' job.

NB: Always keep in mind that sometimes, taking good care of yourself doesn't imply doing lots of things differently as a change of perspective can go a long way in filling your 'personal needs account'. For example, instead of doing chores as if they were painful duties, you can see them as acts of love that you do for your family and yourself. By switching your mindset, you can find some form of enjoyment in everything you do, For example, you can decide to have fun with yourself and the children while you all tidy the house and invent a new song. That in itself can fill your personal needs 'tank' instead of emptying it.

⚒ TOOL #14
Family Culture

Tool co-written with Denise Dampierre – Parenting Coach, HBS alumni and founder of Sosooper.com

Objective: *To become more conscious of the culture you are creating at home while fostering a spirit of family unity and togetherness*

"There's no magic formula for great company culture.
The key is just to treat your staff how
you would like to be treated."
Richard Branson, Founder, Virgin Group

"Culture isn't just one aspect of the game, it is the game.
In the end, an organization is nothing more than
the collective capacity of its people to create value."
Louis Gerstner, former CEO and Chairman of IBM

The beliefs, ideologies, principles and values of an organisation form its culture. An organisation's culture - usually defined in its vision, mission and value statements - creates understanding of the priorities of a business and how to execute them. It therefore strongly influences the way employees behave amongst themselves as well as with people outside the organisation.

Corporate culture is mostly established and defined by senior management; it is something we experience, and rarely create. As we make business decisions, our own leaders inform us of 'the best way to do things here'.

When we come to the leadership position of parent, few of us have intentionally defined or built a culture. We often bring preconceived - and often blurry - assumptions into our family union and these get put to the test when partners act according to their own differing assumptions. This can be amplified when parents come from different cultural backgrounds.

If our priorities and processes are not clear to us, the parents, there is a very high probability they will be fuzzy for our kids. Humble self-scrutiny might even reveal that our actions may not be aligned with the values that we want to instil. For example, what message does shouting angrily, "Be respectful!" really convey?

Jack decides to bring the family together. Having just finished a leadership course and discovered the importance of organisation culture, he is hoping to apply some of these same principles at home:

"So kids, what do you think are the most important values to us as a family?"

"Cake and chocolate!" Kirstie (8) shouts out, laughing.

"Come on Kirstie, you're just being silly, now answer the question properly." Jack replies as Peter (14) offers his own suggestion:

"I think Dad shouldn't be allowed to be so boring all the time."

"Be respectful!" Jack snaps, as Peter sinks back into his seat clearly sulking and mutters:

"This is stupid anyway."

"Fine, forget it then! I don't even know why I bother sometimes", Jack exclaims and marches out of the room in frustration.

How to become a Leader parent

Families, which are also organisations, have a culture that provides a sense of belonging and a 'moral compass' for everyone. It defines desirable behaviour and that which is not. Every family has a culture, whether the parents intend it or not. The good news is that just like a business, a family can change and/or improve their culture at any time.

As Susan David explains in her book Emotional Agility: "Only when kids are properly guided towards learning and trusting their own values can they discover their whys and 'want-to' motivations, the ones that lead to genuine thriving" [23].

A clear family culture helps parents and kids grow together positively. Concise and simple expressions of our family culture such as 'Be kind' can enable toddlers to understand our family values. **Leading by Example (Tool #12)** further helps them translate these ideals into actions.

The key to cooperation and a harmonious family dynamic is to encourage children to adopt an attitude of 'we're all in this together'. In Jack's case, he would have enjoyed better success if he had started this discussion as part of a **Family Meeting** (Tool #22), and if he had sat down with Anna and identified their shared values and the purpose of the discussion before involving the children. By identifying our family culture and values and taking practical steps to achieve our objectives, we are showing them that family life can be a lot more harmonious and enjoyable if everybody plays their part and works together as a team.

When children enter the 'age of reason' (around six), there are several activities that can help make the family culture more relevant and purposeful.

How to set your Family Culture:
Ideas mostly applicable to children aged 6+

1. The first step is to identify with your partner (if you have one) what your values are. This is a particularly useful exercise for couples who come from different cultures, as there can be important differences that are unspoken and it's better to be aware of them. It's important to think about and discuss what is important to you as a family - for example, is exercise and healthy living at the top of your priority list? Or perhaps you are avid readers and wish to instil the same love of words and literature in your children? What qualities/values (such as kindness, curiosity, open mindedness, etc.) would you like your family members to embody?

2. The next step is to sit down with your children and check whether your values are clear to your kids. A fun way to do this is through a 2 Minute Quiz (this is best done as part of a **Family Meeting**, see tool #22):

a) Distribute a pen and paper to everyone with the instructions to list the most important family rules within 2 minutes. (Children too young to write can dictate theirs to parents.). These rules include not only behaviour-related rules that we've set but also values/principles such as 'Be kind', 'Be curious', etc.

b) Then compare and contrast what everyone has written, as this will enable you to *both* explain family values *and* identify how well they are being communicated and understood.

c) During your discussions, you may find that other values will resurge. Make a list of them, e.g. 'Care for self.' 'Care for others.' 'Effort is good.'

3. As your children grow older, you can explain more abstract ideas to them, which may involve:

a) Discussing the concept of having values and what common values you'd like your family to have (for example kindness, curiosity, open-mindedness, etc.). This can include abstract ideas such as wanting to be a family who can trust and be open with one another, and/or more practical ideas such as wanting to eat organic food and exercise more.

b) Having a brainstorming session about what specific actions could instil your key family values in pro-active ways that are both practical and fun. So if for example, you'd like exercise to be a key aspect of your family culture, then agree to go swimming once a week as a family. Or if you walk the kids to school, try power-walking and challenge yourself to improve your time each day.

4. It is engaging and fun to create a visual representation of what these values look like and a great way to do this is using a 'mindmap':

a) For each of your family priorities/values, get the kids involved in creating a diagram to elaborate how each value gets expressed. For example: "What does Effort look like for meals?" could be answered with "Parents cook food and children could help set and clear the table". Or "What could Curiosity taste like at meal times?" could be answered with "Let's eat/cook a meal from a different country every day this week".

b) Commit to doing at least 2 of these activities every week to reinforce your family culture and include this topic as part of weekly family meetings.

c) Take this one step further by creating a 'Family Mission Statement'[24]. This consists of a key statement that describes your family, key qualities/values and how you would like your family to be.

TOOL #15
Family Contribution

Objective: *Developing responsibility and empathy in children and encouraging them to try new things*

"*It takes a lot of people to make a winning team.
Everybody's contribution is important.*"
Gary David Goldberg,
American Writer & Producer for TV & Film

"*Every person has a longing to be significant; to make a contribution; to be a part of something noble and purposeful.*"
John C. Maxwell,
Founder of INJOY, Pastor & Leadership Expert

Contributing and feeling that one has an influence on outcomes/ outputs is a key motivator in the workplace. It gives each team member a sense of purpose and significance, which is crucial to fulfilling their need for self-aspiration. When leaders actively encourage and *allow* people to contribute, particularly when it comes to matters that concern that individual, they are showing each team member that their opinion and input is valued and that they are significant within the business.

As parents, we often expect children to do their fair share of chores, but can present this as an obligation without empowering them and making them want to participate in family life. And when we do allow them to perform age-appropriate tasks, we sometimes can't resist the urge to interfere with advice about how they could do it better, or worse still we swoop in and do the task for them. Sadly, in doing this we are robbing our children of the opportunity to learn from their mistakes and become more competent at the task in question.

Mollie's doing the laundry and asks her daughter, Sasha (8), for some help:

"Right Sasha, I need you to find all the dirty clothes and put them in the washing machine please."

Fifteen minutes pass and Sasha's still dawdling around the house looking for clothes:

"Would you please hurry up, Sasha! It shouldn't take that long; look, I've not got time to mess around, so just let me do it as I'll get it done in half the time."

Once Mollie finishes with the laundry, she asks James (5) to help her lay the table ready for dinner:

"But why have I got to do it? Can't you make Sasha do it instead?" James complains.

"Just do as you are told for once would you, James?"

After dinner, Mollie asks the children to help her load the dishwasher:

"We can't right now mum, we've both got homework", Sasha argues as they try to dash off to their bedrooms.

"I do everything in this house and you can't even help me to load the dishwasher? Do you think the house just magically cleans itself? You both need to start pulling your weight around here, or would you rather live in a complete mess?"

Once we start to involve children in contributing to the running of the household and empowering them to do so with encouragement rather than criticism, we are giving them what they crave the most, which is a sense of purpose and significance. This helps to foster a sense of family involvement, encourages intrinsic motivation and increases a child's confidence in their own ability.

How to become a Leader parent

We need to enable children to understand and practice self-responsibility as much as possible so that they are better equipped to deal with life's challenges. By actively encouraging young children to practice and learn basic life skills (under supervision where necessary) such as cooking, cleaning etc. they will feel a stronger sense of belonging and significance. Encouraging responsibility in this way drastically reduces any inclination they may have to 'mis'behave.

It's important that we resist the urge to interfere too much (even if, like Mollie we feel that they are taking too long) and allow them to make their own (safe) mistakes as they are learning. This process of trial and error is a vital lesson in itself and is so much more valuable than any lessons that they are 'told'.

How to use Family Contribution:

For young children:

1. Give age-appropriate tasks: make sure that you take the time to teach them how to do it properly, and don't make the mistake of expecting children to excel in tasks that they haven't been trained in.

2. Allow them to make mistakes and experience the consequences of their actions: as hard as it can sometimes be, resist the urge to intervene to prevent them from making the mistake or reprimand them for it. (See Tool # 18 - **Mistakes as Opportunities for Learning**).

3. When they do make a mistake (which they invariably will!), help them develop their problem-solving skills by giving them a few alternative ideas of how they could improve the way they approach the task next time and let them choose one of the ideas (see Tool #21 – **Problem Solving**).

4. Where possible, give them the opportunity to do the task again, so that they get a chance to do it 'right'.

For children aged five years and over:

1. A great way to kick start this is to hold a **Family Meeting** (Tool #22) to discuss the importance of everyone contributing to the running of the household.

2. Make a chore list that includes all the tasks that have to be done on a weekly basis (including parental tasks such as driving kids to school and different activities, shopping, etc.). This allows you to highlight to your children just how much time and labour parents contribute to the family and will in itself significantly reduce a child's resistance to doing their fair share.

3. Involve children in creating their chore list by asking them for their ideas and suggestions as to what responsibilities they could take on, whether it be taking out the rubbish, setting the table for mealtimes or cleaning up after meals. This is one of the keys to reducing attention-seeking behaviour as it makes children feel more important.

4. The next step is to make a family agreement about who will do what. If there are any arguments as to who does what (as children can get excited about taking on new tasks when presented this way!), simply remind the children that they'll get the chance to swap or change chores the following week.

5. If your children are reluctant, try to find a more attractive word than 'chores' such as 'home jobs' or 'responsibilities'.

6. Inject some fun into the task at hand by approaching it with a 'whistle while you work' mentality, as this shows kids that chores can be fun and have a useful purpose and aren't simply to be 'got through'.

7. Establish the chores into a routine so that they become a habitual part of everyday life.

How to Lead by Example, Motivate & Inspire

- Lead by example by modelling the behaviours/qualities you would most like to see children adopt such as kindness, empathy, patience, respectfulness, etc.

- Learn to regulate your own emotions so that your children can learn to control theirs.

- Be kind to yourself. Try to avoid falling into common parenting traps such as striving to be the 'perfect parent' or blaming yourself or the children when things go wrong.

- Focus on self-care by ensuring that your own needs are being met. When we take good care of ourselves, we are far better placed to be able to take care of those around us.

- Identify what's important to you all as a family and use these key qualities and values as a way to define your family culture.

- Help children to become more confident and independent by actively encouraging them to practice basic life skills (under supervision where necessary) such as cooking, cleaning, etc. This fosters a spirit of family contribution and helps to increase their sense of belonging and significance.

- Allow children to contribute by involving them in the running of the household; this helps them to understand and practice self-responsibility, encourages intrinsic motivation and increases their confidence in their own ability.

Your Notes

CHAPTER 5

Building Trust & Connection

In corporate life, the connection and trust that we build with our team has a great impact upon our influence as a colleague and leader. Our colleagues and staff are more likely to listen to us, trust us and allow us to influence them when we find ways to connect with them and gain their trust.

We connect with and earn the trust of others by using our emotional intelligence, which entails considering other people's emotions, as well as managing and controlling our own emotions, rather than being reactive. There is no quick fix but the pay-off for being more aware of and in control of one's emotions is huge. It is a crucial step in being an effective, inspiring parent and leader.

In family life, even though we might act with the best of intentions, and our intention as parents is always to have the best possible connection and sense of trust with our children, sometimes the way in which we interact with them can damage this connection.

The tools in this chapter are specifically adapted to show busy working parents how to:

- Make the time you spend with children really 'count'.

- Build a stronger connection with children through Emotion Coaching.

- Make children feel listened to.

 TOOL #16
Presence

Objective: *Building a strong connection with children and in so doing, preventing attention-seeking behaviour and many other issues*

> *"The most valuable commodity of the 21st century will be undivided attention."*
> **Phil Cooke, Writer & Television Producer**

In the workplace, one of the most effective ways of building a stronger sense of trust and connection between colleagues and team members is by giving full and focused attention to each member of the team.

We want our children to feel that we are there for them and are listening to them, but the reality is that we may frequently be busy with other things, and in these cases we are not paying real attention to them. We might be present physically, but so pre-occupied by work or other commitments that we don't realise we aren't giving them the benefit of our full presence and undivided attention.

During these times, we usually give answers to their questions automatically, and don't take the time to read between the lines and really *hear* what they're trying to say. We justify this to ourselves by blaming our lack of time on our busy schedules. Sadly, all of the explanations in the world, however justified, won't stop this lack of quality time together from having a negative impact upon the relationship and connection we have with our children.

Anna is in the kitchen with her son Peter (14):

"So how did the spelling test go in the end? I know you were pretty worried about it this morning."

"Actually, it went much…"

Anna's phone rings and she cuts him off mid-sentence as she answers it. "Just give me a minute Peter – it's work so I have to take this."

Peter waits patiently for Anna to finish her phone call and continues: "The test was actually okay..." he begins.

Anna disappears behind the fridge door to rummage for something for dinner, "Yes, go on Peter", she says when she re-emerges with a handful of carrots.

Peter keeps talking as Anna chops carrots, but soon gives up and leaves.

How to become a Leader parent

Just as giving our colleagues our focused attention helps to build trust in the workplace, being fully 'present' with our children is one of the most powerful ways of building a deep and long-lasting connection with them. To create a strong emotional bond with our children, we need to spend quality time with them. This time needs to be separate from usual obligations such as homework and household chores as they come with their own set of challenges.

This isn't always easy, particularly in families where both parents are working and have more than one child, as there are so many other commitments to consider. We can however, make the most of the time we do get to spend with them by communicating effectively to make sure that we reduce power struggles (see **Chapter 2**), and by being fully present and giving them our undivided attention. It is also important to schedule some regular one-on-one time with each child as this fills up their 'emotional bank account' and their need for love and belonging.

This tool is a great way to prevent kids from misbehaving and having tantrums as it helps to build a strong connection between parent and child and shows them that we value and cherish them. It is also particularly suitable for addressing sibling rivalry, because scheduling in regular one-to-one time with each child stops them from feeling as though they have to compete for time and attention.

How to be fully present with your children:

- To really enjoy spending special time with your children relies on being fully present and giving them full and undivided attention. Of course, there are times when this simply isn't possible. So, if like Anna, you're in the middle of doing something else, rather than listening to kids with half an ear, you can tell them:

  "I'd love to spend time with you, but I really need to get dinner started, grab a carrot and help me do this and then we'll sit down with a hot chocolate and I'll be all ears".
  Peter is far more likely to want to open up to Anna again in future if he knows that she is willing to make the time to listen to him.

- Lead by example – the most effective way to show children the importance of focussed undivided attention is by modelling this behaviour yourself. This not only encourages children to open up and talk, but it also increases the likelihood that they will listen to what you have to say in return. By encouraging them to become active listeners, you are also equipping them with essential life skills that will continue to be of great benefit as they grow to become adults.

- It's important to schedule in some regular one-on-one time with each child by following the steps below:

  1. At the beginning of a day or a week, schedule some time to dedicate to each child individually.

  2. For children younger than five, schedule around ten minutes of 'special time' every day - which can be tricky with more than two children. With children older than five, try it less regularly, but for longer periods. Try to schedule at least 30 minutes once a week.

  3. At the beginning of the session, say: "This is our special time together" to make sure that they value it.

  4. Offer a choice of two or three of your child's favourite activities to do together. It could be sitting together to

read, cook, draw (most children love drawing with their parents), go for a walk, do a puzzle, play cards etc.

NB: We strongly recommend that your activity includes playing, as this is something that we don't usually have enough time to do with our children. Not only does this fulfil their need for Fun and Play, but it is also one of the key ways they learn essential life skills, particularly when they are younger[25]. It's also important to let children 'lead us' in the game that they choose.

TOOL #17
Emotion Coaching

Objective: *Teaching children how to cope with and regulate their emotions*

> *"When people can't control their own emotions,*
> *they have to control someone else's behaviour."*
> **John Cleese, Comedian, Actor, Writer & Film Producer**

> *"When you show deep empathy toward others,*
> *their defensive energy goes down, and positive energy replaces it.*
> *That's when you can get more creative in solving problems."*
> **Stephen Covey - Best-Selling Author of**
> **'7 Habits of Highly Effective People'**

The ability to connect with people on a meaningful level by using empathy and active listening is a powerful leadership skill. Listening to other people and accepting their emotional reactions, whether in agreement with them or not, demonstrates an ability to understand and relate to what they are going through.

Often we don't really 'hear' what our partner or our children are trying to tell us, when we're busy trying to deal with a million other things at once. With our children, instead of actively listening to what they want to say and acknowledging their feelings, we often either dismiss what they are trying to tell us, or we swoop in with reassurances to try to fix the problem for them.

It's only natural that we should want to protect them from anger, hurt and frustration, and our intention is usually to help them get rid of their anxiety. However, by offering constant reassurances and using phrases such as "Come on, it's not that bad" or by giving them solutions to their problems, we are inadvertently making our children feel that their feelings are being discounted. We are also sending them the message that upset, disappointment and frustration must be avoided at all costs.

Denying or minimising feelings gives children the message that some feelings are shameful or unacceptable. As children at a young age cannot differentiate between their emotions and their 'selves', they can interiorise that they are not ok. Moreover, when we deny people's feelings, the logical parts of their brain can shut down so it makes it more difficult to connect with them.

In the long-term, kids are less likely to trust what we say if all we offer is constant reassurances in the face of their problems. No matter how many times we tell them that "Everything's going to be okay", if they believe the contrary, then no amount of reassurance from a well-meaning parent is going to change that.

Julia is busy cooking dinner, when her daughter, Annabelle (3), trips over a shoe that's been left on the hallway floor, and immediately starts to wail:

"Don't make such a fuss, Annabelle. I saw you fall, it wasn't that bad!"

Annabelle doesn't take any notice of her mother and starts to scream even louder. John storms down from upstairs wanting to know what's causing the commotion. Seeing Annabelle still crying on the floor, without hesitation he crouches down and asks:

"Why are you crying?"

"I fell and hurt myself", answers Annabelle sobbing.

"Oh darling, you poor little thing – I promise that everything is going to be okay. Now how about I get you some of your favourite sweets, would that make you feel better?"

Annabelle's tears disappear in an instant:

"Yes Daddy, or maybe an ice cream?"

In the case where children come to us with a specific issue, e.g. when a child says that they hate school, it sometimes isn't school itself that's causing the issue. It may be that they are struggling to make friends or that they are having difficulty with one of their subjects. Therefore, by automatically offering advice and reassurances, we may miss out on an invaluable opportunity to 'meet our children where they are', to connect with them and teach them essential problem-solving skills.

If we don't connect with them, listen to them in a non-judgemental way and try to 'hear' what isn't said, we may fail to understand the root cause of their behaviour. When this happens, we address the symptoms rather than the cause and might take actions that serve only to make the problem worse instead of solving it. And in doing so, we risk losing their trust and the connection we have with them.

How to become a Leader parent

Connecting with children on an emotional level vastly increases the likelihood of them cooperating with us and wanting to do as we ask. Because when we appeal to the right side of their brain - the part of the brain responsible for feelings - their emotional needs feel met and they are much more capable of redirecting their emotions and/or behaviour.

It is therefore important that we listen and validate our children's feelings by practising empathy (see more on how to do this below) in order to connect with them. Connecting with our children in this way will help them learn how to deal with unpleasant or challenging emotions so that they grow to trust themselves and their reactions in the long-term. It will also help them learn how to self-regulate their emotions.

Some parents resist giving empathy because they worry that this might reinforce the child's attitude and/or behaviour. This has some truth to it as for instance, allowing a child to wallow in their feelings and feeling sorry or pity for them, as John did in the example above, can reinforce the behaviour. Empathy here is used in the sense of conveying to our children that, "Although I may not know/understand what you are experiencing, I recognise that you are feeling strong emotions".

Empathy is about acknowledging our children's emotions and feelings but not conveying that the ensuing behaviour or self-pitying is ok. So as parents, we can empathise with the fact that there must be a reason behind our children's behaviour, while making it clear that this doesn't justify acting out in any way they want to.

Other parents have difficulty giving empathy because they weren't given much of it when they were children, and they may therefore be uncomfortable around strong emotions. In this case, their 'instinctive' reaction will be to reassure or minimise their children's feelings. Following the steps below will allow you to practise giving empathy and incorporate it in your daily life for your benefit and that of your children.

How to use Emotion Coaching:

Listening is the basis of empathy, and children feel validated and more understood when they feel listened to without judgement and aren't immediately given well-meaning advice. In other words, when we refrain from passing judgement and giving advice, children know that we have no agenda beyond being there for them.

Therefore, when children show a strong emotion (such as crying or throwing a tantrum) or share negative or distressed feelings (e.g. "I have no friends" or "I hate school"), **you should avoid**:

- **Denying their feelings** or trying to save them from unpleasant or challenging emotions. Julia may have thought that she was being helpful by trying to stop Annabelle from crying. However, it's better to avoid reassuring children with phrases such as "It's going to be okay," or "It's not that bad" or try to stem their emotions with "Calm down", "Stop crying" or "Only babies cry". These reactions have the effect of discounting their feelings and can cause their brain to 'shut down'.

- **Ignoring your child**. This can send them the message that you do not care and it will usually lead to the situation escalating, as they will want your attention. That said, it can be ok to temporarily ignore a child's tantrum after you've connected with them and acknowledged their feelings (see steps below).

- **Asking "Why are you crying?"**, even if you have no idea what is causing their emotional distress. This is a difficult question for a child to answer, and asking them does not help them to understand or process their emotions. In general, avoid being too logical until you connect with them (see below), as you can make it more difficult for a child experiencing intense emotions to be able to connect with you.

- **Interrupting them to offer a solution** to immediately 'solve' their problem and calm their emotions as John does in the example above. This doesn't allow them to learn how to process their feelings and develop their 'frustration muscle'. So if your child breaks something or their ice cream has fallen on the floor, you can give them empathy but should avoid immediately offering to buy them a new one.

- **Pressuring them** by making statements such as, "You're obviously upset about something - you have to tell me what it is so I can help you", instead you can try, "You seem upset about something, do you want to talk about it?".

Steps to Emotion Coaching:

I. **Your child is having a strong emotion**, such as a tantrum or crying because they've hurt themselves:

1. **Connect with them:** The best way to do this is to appeal first to the right side of their brain, to help engage them into a more receptive state of mind. To do this, use a soft tone of voice, get down to their level and if the circumstances allow, give them a hug. A hug is one of the most effective ways of redirecting a child's emotions because studies show that when we hug someone, this stimulates the brain's production of dopamine and oxytocin, which help to reduce stress and promote a feeling of happiness and relaxation.

2. **Acknowledge and Name their feelings:** Children feel validated and accepted when we acknowledge their perspective and help them to name what they are feeling. They aren't equipped to be able to understand, acknowledge or explain

their feelings, so you can help them by trying to read their body language. By helping them put a name to what they are feeling, you are enabling them to 'own' their emotions and therefore control them. In situations like this, words are incredibly empowering because they normalise the unknown into something knowable, tangible and therefore manageable. Dan Siegel, famous neuroscientist calls this: 'Name it to tame it' [26]. So for example:

a) When children are upset or throwing a tantrum: "You seem really frustrated and angry", "You seem to be having a lot of trouble coping with what I just told you" or "You're so disappointed that your friend is not sharing his/her toys with you."

b) When children hurt themselves: "Oh, that seems to have hurt!" or "You look like you're in pain."

3. **Help them redirect their emotions:** After taking the above steps, help your child to redirect their emotions by doing the following:

a) When your child is upset and throwing a tantrum, give them a choice. For example, "Would you like to come to the park with me or stay here on the floor?"

b) When your child is hurt: "Do you need help getting up or can you do it yourself?" or "Does that hurt a lot, average or just a little?"

c) When upset with a friend or sibling try: "Fighting won't solve anything, if I were in your shoes I'd try using words instead."

d) In most other situations simply ask: "Is there something that I can do to help?"

f) Use laughter: Be cautious when doing this because you don't want them to feel that you are minimising their feelings by laughing at a situation or what they are feeling. Yet using humour to make them see things from a different perspective can sometimes help as it releases hormones than will help to calm things down.

e) If you haven't already done it, give them a hug (see above for benefits of hugs).

II. Your child is expressing a negative emotion, such as 'I have no friends' or "I hate school"

1. **Actively listen:** Try sitting at your child's side, shoulder-to-shoulder as eye-to-eye contact can make it more difficult for children to feel comfortable enough to share, and then do the following:

   a) Repeat what your child is saying or rephrase it, so for e.g. "You feel you have no friends", or "You seem sad because you think you have no friends?";

   b) Remember not to try to 'fix' the problem and instead, validate their feelings with empathy by describing how you think your child might be feeling (see point 2 above). For example "That sounds painful…", or "Sounds like you are feeling upset…".

   c) Do not 'exaggerate' their feelings (i.e. try to use the same tone as they are using and do not use superlatives) as this could make them doubt your sincerity.

2. **Problem-Solve:** Active Listening will help your child to process their emotions, and will often be enough for them to get rid of their negative feelings. However, in some cases they may be coming to you with an issue that they would like you to offer direct support on. In these cases, once you have really heard everything that they have to say, you can use the tool **Problem Solving (#21)**, to coach them into finding their own solutions to the challenges they encounter.

III. Your child is whining or arguing, and isn't expressing an important need (food, sleep, warmth, etc.).

1. **Acknowledge their desire**, and use **Positive Redirection** (see Tool #9) whenever possible. For example, "You really want to have some cake, and you can have some after dinner".

2. **Use an empathetic statement to stay detached**: If Positive Redirection hasn't stopped the whining, it's important not to get sucked into an argument. It's much better to try to diffuse their reaction without getting too emotionally involved, as this would makes it more likely that we will get angry or give in. To remain emotionally detached from the situation, select an empathetic statement such as "I hear you" or "I know" or simply "Oh…" and keep repeating it every time your childs whines or argues to get something you are not willing to give them.

3. **Remain consistent and do not give in**: It's important to be as consistent as possible and not give in so that your child learns that they cannot get what they want when they whine and argue. After using this technique a few times, and provided you used the same empathetic statement consistently, your child is likely to stop whining and arguing as soon as you start using this technique. Indeed, children are 'energy efficient' and they soon realise that they won't get what they want once they hear this statement.

Further examples for solving typical parenting challenges

1. Child refusing or making a fuss over homework

"There seems to be something that's worrying you about your homework this week. Would you like to have a chat about it before you start working?"

2. Child arguing and negotiating

"I hear that you would like to go to your friend's place and you can do this after finishing your homework". And if they start arguing and negotiating, you can repeat "I hear you" or "I know" in a calm tone of voice without giving in, until they stop arguing.

3. Child throwing a tantrum

For more ideas on how to deal with Tantrums, you can download our short eBook from Amazon: *Tantrums: A Step-by-Step Guide to Preventing and Diffusing Your Child's Outbursts.*

How to Build Trust & Connection

- Being truly present and giving undivided attention helps build a strong sense of trust and connection between parent and child, so schedule in regular special one-on-one time with each child.

- Allow children to express themselves, particularly when they are faced with difficult or challenging emotions - having their feelings heard and accepted is an essential part of children learning how to trust their emotions and self-regulate.

- Acknowledging a child's perspective and helping them to name what they are feeling enables them to 'own' their emotions, which makes them better equipped to control and regulate their emotions in the long-term.

- When a child comes to us with a problem, it's important that we try to avoid swooping in with reassurances or try to fix the problem for them as this can make them feel that their feelings are discounted.

- Try to 'hear' the hidden messages behind what children are saying, and when they do start to open up, don't interrupt them and refrain from judgement.

- Do not give in to whining or nagging behaviour as this will just reinforce this behaviour. Avoid getting sucked into an argument and doing too much explaining by using an empathetic statement such as 'I know' to diffuse the situation instead.

Your Notes

CHAPTER 6

Allowing Children to be Accountable for Their Actions

In corporate life, we are accountable for our actions and we understand that our job may be on the line if we don't deliver. Yet, in family life, we cannot fire our children and our children cannot fire us. This simple fact completely changes the nature of accountability, and it allows for some situations that would be unthinkable in the workplace.

We are our children's guides and they need to learn from the time they spend with us how to deal with the 'real' world. They should therefore learn to be accountable and responsible for their actions as this will help them to become increasingly independent as they grow older.

There are key things that we can do to improve our children's ability to be able to learn from their mistakes, encourage them to behave better and help them to become more responsible for their actions.

This chapter will equip you with tools that will allow you to:

- Increase the likelihood that children will learn from their mistakes.

- Replace conventional forms of punishment with a more effective alternative that makes children accountable for their actions and teaches them how to behave better, without damaging the connection you have with them.

⚙ TOOL #18
Mistakes as Opportunities for Learning

Objective: Empowering children by teaching them how to embrace their mistakes

---

"If you're not making mistakes, then you're not doing anything. I'm positive that a doer makes mistakes."
John Wooden, American Basketball Player & Coach

"Experience is making mistakes and learning from them."
Bill Ackman, Founder & CEO of
Pershing Square Capital Management LP

When mistakes happen in the workplace, the best leaders allow team members the space to reflect upon, and ultimately learn from, the mistake they have made, without 'forcing the learning' onto them. They also provide a 'safe' environment so that team members feel comfortable to take risks and make mistakes because they recognise that his is an essential part of the learning process.

Google recently released its findings on 'Project Aristotle'; its objective was to look for what makes a great team and what leaders can do to provide a better environment for teams to thrive. After years of analysis on its tens of thousands of employees, they discovered that the first key was 'safety'. We're all reluctant to engage in behaviours that could negatively influence how others perceive our competence, awareness, and positivity. Although this kind of self-protection is a natural strategy in the workplace, it is detrimental to effective teamwork. The safer team members feel with one another, the more likely they are to admit mistakes, to partner, and to take on new roles, which makes for a more united and effective team.

This is the same with parenting. Safety is paramount for a child to feel comfortable in making mistakes. Parents usually provide this safety without a second thought, particularly when children are younger, by preparing their environment to provide safety and by offering positive body language, smiles, upbeat encouragement and other emotional triggers. However, some of our reactions as parents (e.g. when we overreact to our children's mistakes and misbehaviour and/or get angry) can create a fear in children and make them afraid of making mistakes (see **Growth Mindset** – Tool #20).

That said, it's important to remember, that making it safe for children to make mistakes does not mean that we should be over-protecting them. As parents, it's totally natural to want to protect our children from the bad things in life. We may therefore find ourselves swooping in and 'rescuing' them from challenging situations. Whilst we may have the best of intentions, what we are often doing (unless there is real danger) is robbing children of the opportunity to learn the invaluable lessons that making mistakes and the process of trial and error has to teach.

Even worse, when we repeatedly issue children with warnings of all the bad things that may happen, we can make them anxious about life's dangers. We inadvertently disempower them by showing them that we are not prepared to trust them and have no faith in their ability to cope with/learn from making mistakes. Phrases such as "I told you so", only serve to distance them further away from taking responsibility for their mistake and/or learning from its natural consequences, and makes children less inclined to listen to what we have to say.

Anna is about to drop Peter (14) off at the school gates, when Peter realises that he's forgotten to bring his lunch box for the school field trip that day:

"What am I going to do? I'll be starving if I don't have any lunch, and I can't go back and get it now because I'll be late for assembly and get a detention. Can't you quickly drive home and get it for me?"

"Fine, but just this once okay?" Anna drives home, grabs Peter's lunch box and ends up making herself late for work.

After work, she takes Chloe to the park and hovers over her daughter as she runs around playing:

"Be careful Chloe, you're going to fall over if you keep running so fast!"

"Chloe, be more careful! You're going to hurt yourself if you don't watch where you're going!"

"Be careful of those stinging nettles!" Anna warns and leads her daughter away to a different part of the park ...

How to become a Leader parent

Every childhood experience, if handled well, can become an invaluable learning experience. Allowing children to make mistakes and experience their natural consequences teaches them that it's ok to get things wrong from time to time. And as a result they will become better equipped, not only at handling their mistakes, but also at preventing them in the long-term.

So what to do instead, however hard it may be, is to start learning to identify which mistakes we need to allow children to make. Such mistakes are known as 'affordable' mistakes (as opposed to 'unaffordable' mistakes that could result in serious upset or injury). And by allowing children to deal with the 'natural', i.e. the immediate and logical consequences of their mistakes, means that they become much better at finding ways to solve them in the long-term.

The key is also how we deal with our own mistakes. We can demonstrate that it is important to embrace mistakes by modelling this behaviour when we make one ourselves. And we need to try to resist the urge to swoop in and try to rescue them from frustration and disappointment, and instead allow them the opportunity to train their 'disappointment muscles'. As parents, it's important that we have faith in our children and believe that they can survive upset and disappointment because they will become more confident and resilient in the process.

How to allow children to make mistakes and learn from them:

When you see a child in a situation where they might hurt themselves, drop something or are doing something that may cause themselves harm:

1. Explain what you would do in their situation, and mention what the natural consequences to their actions might be. For example, "If I were you, I'd slow down a bit on your scooter because if it goes too fast, you may lose control and end up hurting yourself".

2. However difficult it may be, if they refuse to listen, you need to allow them to make the mistake and face the natural consequences of their actions. In this case, it would mean allowing them to fall off of their scooter, providing they're in a safe environment (or in this case wearing a helmet) and there was no risk of serious harm or injury.

3. In the event that they do hurt themselves, resist the urge to say, "I told you so!" as this puts the focus on our warning rather than the child's decision, and the opportunity for learning is therefore lost. Such a reaction, although completely natural in any parent as we are just trying to save our children pain and discomfort by giving them the benefit of our own experiences, is actually akin to - unintentional - shaming. It can provoke rebellion, rather than having the desired effect of inspiring improvement. Mistakes only become opportunities for learning when we allow our children to take responsibility for them.

4. Respond with empathy instead, to connect with your child (See Tool #17 - **Emotion Coaching**). You can give them a hug and acknowledge their feelings. For example: "That must hurt!".

5. Allow children to redirect their emotions by asking them questions such as: "Does it hurt a lot, or just a little?", or "Is there anything I can do to help?"

6. Later when they are calm, you can try sharing stories of some of the mistakes that you have made, and how you sought to fix them. This is a great way of showing children that we are all human and are all prone to making mistakes from time to time.

7. If you feel that you child is generally afraid of making mistakes, you could take this one step further and invite each

member of the family to share a mistake 'of the day' or 'of the week', and ask what they have learnt from it. (This is something that you could add to the agenda in your **Family Meetings**, see Tool #22).

The more that you show respect for other family members for admitting and solving their mistakes, the more your children will understand that there is a positive, learning aspect to getting things wrong. It's much better to start implementing this with children when they are young (from the age of four) so that by the time they are older it will have become a habit, and they will know how to embrace mistakes and learn from them.

✖ TOOL #19
Logical and Delayed Consequences

Objective: Finding a more effective alternative to disciplining children that makes them accountable for their actions and develops their sense of responsibility.

"Accountability breeds response-ability."
Stephen Covey, Best-Selling Author of
'7 Habits of Highly Effective People'

"The key to successful leadership is influence, not authority."
Kenneth H. Blanchard, Author of
'Leadership and the One Minute Manager'

Holding people accountable for their actions is an essential aspect of leadership in the corporate world as it ensures that team members follow the rules and fulfil the expectations of them, and ultimately leads to better performance.

At home, there seems to be many conflicting theories about how to discipline children and ensure that they behave well. As developmental psychologist Gordon Neufeld explains, there is actually often too much emphasis on discipline: "Many people think that discipline is the essence of parenting. But that isn't parenting. Parenting is providing the conditions in which a child can realize his or her full human potential." [27]

The word 'discipline' comes from the Latin 'disciplina', which means teaching, learning and giving instruction, so disciplining effectively means 'to teach'. The most common way to discipline children is to punish them. Punishment is based on the premise that in order to make sure children remember that they shouldn't repeat a behaviour, they must feel some kind of discomfort or pain.

Although punishment may improve a child's behaviour, a plethora of research now shows that this change in behaviour is only temporary and that there is a long list of potential negative consequences of punishing. Indeed, children who are regularly punished will only comply with their parent's instructions and requests out of fear, so the effect is only short-term.

In the long-term, punishment not only damages the relationship and connection between parent and child, but it can also cause them to become resentful and increasingly aggressive. And in many cases, they will learn to lie and hide things as a means of avoiding future punishment[28]. Punishment is therefore an entirely negative experience that breeds feelings of shame and resentment, and can actually make future behaviour worse[29].

Another issue with punishment is that we often react in the 'heat of the moment', in the belief that we must do something immediately to make children realise their misdeeds. So we end up 'blurting out' threats or punishments that are totally unrelated to the deed and that may not have the intended effect.

Mollie and her children have recently moved house; she parks her car in the driveway and sees that James (5) is at the front door, with what looks like a screwdriver in his hand:

"James, what are you doing?" She calls out as she approaches the house. James seems to suddenly freeze, as if caught in the act. As she gets closer, she sees that he has dug holes into the wooden front door with a screwdriver.

"I can't believe what I'm seeing! What on earth do you think you're doing? What am I going to do with you?! You're forbidden from using the iPad for the next five, no ... ten days!"

James looks at her with a mixed look of part fear and part relief, and then exhales loudly before candidly saying: "Ten days Mummy? Really? Only ten days? Thanks Mummy, thanks!"

Children are not always as candid as James was in the above example! Had he not have expressed relief when hearing the punishment, Mollie may have still thought that this punishment was going to teach him a lesson.

In these heated moments, we are actually more likely to threaten our children with much stronger punishments out of anger. However, we may fail to follow through on such threats because we soon realise that they are impractical or too harsh for the deed in question. Unfortunately, issuing empty threats only serves to undermine our parental authority in the long-term.

On the occasions when we do follow through, if we implement a punishment that is unrelated to their misbehaviour, it is more likely to breed hostility and resentment than teach children a valuable lesson about responsibility and being accountable. Implementing unrelated consequences in this way casts Mum/Dad in the role of 'bad guy' and makes the child angry and resentful towards their parent rather than realising what they should've done better, which is hardly a motivation for the child to improve in the long-term.

It's also very difficult for children to understand that every action has a logical consequence if the punishment that we choose to implement has no relation to their misbehaviour. And if they don't understand the link between action and consequence, then they are more likely to repeat the misbehaviour in future.

As Jane Nelsen, founder of Positive Discipline[30] puts so well: "Where did we ever get the crazy idea that in order to make children do better, first we have to make them feel worse? Think of the last time you felt humiliated or treated unfairly. Did you feel like cooperating or doing better?"

So if punishment doesn't work, how do we make children accountable for their behaviour and 'teach' them to want to do better?

How to become a Leader parent

The premise is very similar to what we learn from leadership, which is that in order to want to do better, people need to be made to feel good and better about themselves, rather than feel pain and discomfort.

To achieve this, we need to move away from conventional punishment and 'blame and shame' and try instead to understand the root cause of a child's behaviour, and first address their needs for control, autonomy and significance (see Chapters 2 and 3 for tools that will address these needs).

Even when we address these needs, children are likely to still feel the need to test the boundaries. In this case, we should make children accountable for their actions by imposing Logical Consequences that are related to a child's misbehaviour. This teaches them that every choice they make in life has a consequence.

However, in some cases, we may not be in a position to deliver a Logical Consequence: we are either too angry and cannot think of an appropriate consequence or cannot implement it (for example if we're in the car).

When faced with children's misbehaviour, parents usually react immediately in the belief that a consequence is more effective if it's delivered right away. The issue is that in these circumstances, the prefrontal cortex can 'shut down' and our body can become flooded with hormones that prevent us from thinking rationally. So we may end up issuing threats or punishments without having enough time to think about whether they are reasonable and whether we are able to follow through on them.

During these reactionary moments, it's better to refrain from intervening as this often causes the situation to escalate. From the age of three or four, children have enough of a memory to understand and relate to the consequences that we implement in the future. It is therefore better to apply a Delayed Consequence (see steps below) in these circumstances.

In Mollie's example above, as she was so angered by her son's behaviour, she could have delayed her consequence rather than dish out an unrelated punishment that did not have the intended effect at all.

Logical and Delayed Consequences are more effective than punishment because they:

- Don't focus on blaming or shaming the child and instead focus on following the rules of the three R's, so **the consequences are:**
  - ○ **Related** to the child's misbehaviour
  - ○ **Respectful**
  - ○ **Reasonable**

- Are delivered with love, empathy and without anger.

- Focus on the poor choice, i.e. the behaviour, rather than the 'bad' or 'naughty' child.

- Are not accompanied by lectures, 'I told you so's' or shaming.

- Are not accompanied by lots of explanations and justifications for the decisions we have made as this just gives children more opportunity to argue with them.

- Teach children wisdom by making their decision/mistake the 'bad guy' rather than the parent handing out the punishment.

So rather than feel shamed or singled out, children become more aware of the impact that their behaviour has on those around them. The long-term effect of this is quite profound because a child who understands that every action has a natural and logical consequence is more likely to develop an intrinsic motivation to behave well, rather than being motivated to only behave well out of fear.

How to use Logical Consequences:

If your child breaks a rule that you have set (refer to Tool #11 - **Setting Rules and Clarifying Expectations**), and you are in a position to deliver a logical consequence (i.e. not too angry, in the car, etc.):

1. **Think of a Logical Consequence** that you can impose and that follows the three R's rule. So for example if your child

has made a mess, a respectful, reasonable and related consequence would be to make them clean up the mess themselves (see many other examples below).

2. **Deliver it with empathy**: when you impose the consequence, you should try as much as possible - and it is often challenging to do when we're angry - to show empathy when delivering it. As explained in **Emotion Coaching** (Tool #17), it's much more difficult for children to learn if you haven't connected with them first. You should also show that you have hope in your child's ability to control their behaviour in future. So instead of: "I told you three times to pick your clothes up off the floor and that you won't be going to the park until they are... the clothes are still there so we're not going!", try: "This is so sad, I really wanted to take you to the park today, but you'll have to stay home and tidy all those clothes up off the floor".

3. **Do not give lots of explanations or give in**: once the consequence is delivered be consistent, do not give lots of explanations - as otherwise this can lead children to think that they can 'out-negotiate' you, so 'stick to your guns'. The only exception being if the consequence did not follow the three R's. In this case, simply explain to your child that you made a mistake and acted in the heat of the moment and that you will think of a more appropriate consequence.

4. **Later on, do a problem-solving session:** if your child is older than three, you can do use **Problem Solving** (see Tool #21) to make sure the behaviour doesn't reoccur. This should be done at least an hour after the event to ensure both you and your child have settled down.

NB: Why the 'Naughty step' and Time-out should be replaced by 'Time away':

If your child is wound up and/or you are angered by their behaviour (e.g. if they hit you or one of their siblings or friends), the best way to stop the situation from escalating is to remove them from the situation and put them in another room (preferably their bedroom). In these cases, it is very important to remember not to make this a punishment, and it is far easier said than done. In order to achieve this, avoid labelling children 'naughty' (as this is labelling the person rather than the behaviour), and use empathy when explaining to children that they're going to have to take some time away as they need to calm down. So for example, you can say with as much empathy as you can - taking into consideration the circumstances and without lecturing: "Uh-oh, it seems like you need a bit of Time-Away to calm down".

This is a logical consequence that is directly related to the circumstances. And to make sure your child understand how it is related to the event, you should ideally explain to your child beforehand that when things get out of control, it is important to be able to take some time away to calm down. You could also mention that adults also sometimes need some time away when they get wound up.

Once your child has calmed down, you should wait a little moment to give them time to process the situation and then ask them if they're ready to come back. If they are, welcome them back with a hug and without lots of explanations for what happened. If your child is older than three, you can then do a problem-solving session later on.

How to use Delayed Consequences:

There is a significant difference between *reacting* and *responding* when faced with conflict or power struggles. When we react rather than respond to a child's misbehaviour, we can do or say things that may be regretted later. When children 'push our buttons', it's only natural to feel annoyed, upset or frustrated - these feelings only become problematic when they cloud judgement.

Therefore, using Delayed Consequences is much more effective because it helps to reduce much of the anger, fear and resentment (in both parent and child) that are the inevitable result of trying to deal with a child's misbehaviour 'on the spot'. Instead of labelling a child as 'bad' or 'naughty', waiting allows us to make a sensible decision about what consequences we are going to apply.

Responding in a rational and measured way and implementing consequences from a place of reason encourages children to take responsibility for their mistakes so that they are far less likely to repeat them. This tool is also useful for when we cannot act straightaway to a child's misbehaviour, such as when in a car.

Key steps to Delayed Consequences:

1. Imagine that you're in the car and your children are fighting in the back seat, but because you are in a hurry you are unable to park the car to wait for them to stop. Instead of threatening children with all sorts of potential punishments, use an empathetic statement: "This is a real shame", or "This is so sad", or simply "Ohh…"

   Follow this empathetic statement with: "I'm going to have to do something about this, but not now…" or "This is not ok, but I'm too angry right now to decide what I'm going to do about this…"

   Another useful alternative is to say: "This behaviour is giving me an energy drain, so I'll have to deal with this later." This shows kids that they will be held accountable for their actions, while removing much of the stress that parents feel when they have to deal with misbehaviour immediately. Using the term 'energy drain' also helps children to understand the impact their behaviour has on those around them.

2. Once the opportunity to illustrate your point arises (it can be up to a week after the event depending on the children's age), tell the children something along the lines of: "Remember when (I had an energy drain because) you wouldn't stop fighting in the back of the car? Well sadly as a result, I'm not going to be able to take you to the theme park today". If you deliver the consequence with empathy, without any hint of 'revenge' and without lecturing, relating it as closely as possible to the original misbehaviour, children will understand that this consequence is a natural and logical one, rather than a punitive punishment.

Further examples for solving typical parenting challenges

1. Child refusing to cooperate

"Sadly, since you haven't tidied your room, you are going to have to stay and tidy it now rather than going to your friend's house."
Or delayed: "You remember how I said I would keep the toys I picked up if you didn't tidy your room? Well, it's such a shame, but I had to pick them up." (and they won't be able to play with them for a few days).

2. Child not doing homework

"It's a shame, but as you haven't done your homework, I'm going to have to switch off the TV."
Or delayed: "Unfortunately, as you didn't finish your homework last time because you were watching TV/playing on the tablet, you cannot use screens today."

3. Child not listening/Ignoring you

"Sadly, because you have chosen not to listen to me, I'm not going to be able to play with you right now."
Or delayed: "I am not feeling listened to and that is draining my energy". And later on: "Remember the energy drain that I had because you didn't listen to me, well I no longer have enough energy to take you to the park."

4. Whining

"I know that you want an ice cream, but sadly the rule in this house is that children who whine cannot get what they are asking for."
Or delayed: "Sadly, since you carried on whining at me in the car I now don't feel like watching our TV programme together."
Or: "All this whining is causing me an energy drain, I'll need your help getting some energy back."

5. Child disrespecting house rules

If a child makes a mess (e.g. spills something, their toys are all over the place etc.): they need to clean/tidy up.

If a child breaks something out of carelessness: they have to pay for it. If they are too young and don't receive pocket money, they can pay it with toys (we could for example take some toys away and give them to charity).

Or delayed: "Sadly, as you've eaten sweets for breakfast this morning when you know you're not supposed to, you won't be able to eat sweets at all for the next few days."

How to Allow Children to be Accountable for Their Actions

- Provide a supportive environment where children feel safe to make mistakes.

- Allow children to make 'affordable' mistakes and resist the urge to swoop in and try to rescue them from frustration and disappointment.

- Show children how important it is to embrace mistakes by modelling this behaviour - this shows them that if handled well, mistakes can be invaluable opportunities for learning.

- Avoid using conventional punishment and instead try to understand the root cause of children's 'mis'behaviour.

- Replace traditional forms of punishment with relevant/logical consequences that are respectful, reasonable and related to children's misbehaviour.

- When children 'mis'behave and we are unable to deal with it immediately, we can implement consequences at a later time.

- Avoid reacting to child's 'mis'behaviour when emotions are affecting your judgement - this allows you to make a more sensible decision later on about what consequences you apply to make children truly accountable for their actions.

Your Notes

Your Notes

CHAPTER 7

Fulfilling Children's Potential

In corporate life, we are used to developing our skills and that of our collaborators. Our objective is to fulfil our potential and that of our team because it helps us, the team and the company as a whole thrive.

As parents, we all want to raise happy and confident children who thrive. We often schedule a plethora of activities so that our children will be happy, acquire knowledge and learn new things. And yet as we shall explore in this chapter, while it's good to have aspirations for our children, it's important to remember that the way in which we choose to guide them towards fulfilling these aspirations can have a profound effect on their attitude towards learning and developing new skills. It can affect not only their willingness to learn, but also their attitude towards their *ability* to learn.

Encouraging them to develop a Growth Mindset (named after Carol Dweck's work[31]), as opposed to a Fixed Mindset, will ensure that they grow to have a healthy level of self-esteem. It will also help them to realise that they have the power to change things and develop their skills in order to become motivated and fulfilled individuals.

Empowering children and involving them in finding solutions to their own challenges and mistakes allows them to become responsible and stand on their own two feet in the short and longer-term.

However, this requires guidance and training as it isn't something that comes naturally.

Thankfully, there is quite a lot that we can learn from the parenting and leadership best practices to guide and train children towards fulfilling their potential and improve our parenting as a whole. In this chapter, we will explore how to:

- Help children develop and nurture their confidence, resilience and self-esteem by encouraging them to adopt a Growth Mindset.

- Empower kids by helping them to find solutions to their own problems and those of the wider family.

- Nurture the idea of family being a team and foster a spirit of unity and togetherness.

⊗ TOOL #20
Growth Mindset

Objective: To build children's self-esteem and strengthen their resilience

> *"Think twice before you speak, because your words and influence will plant the seed of either success or failure in the mind of another."*
> **Napoleon Hill, Author of 'The Law of Success'**

> *"If parents want to give their children a gift, the best thing they can do is to teach them to love challenges, be intrigued by mistakes, enjoy effort, and keep on learning. That way, their children don't have to be slaves of praise. They will have a lifelong way to build and repair their own confidence."*
> **Carol S. Dweck, Lewis and Virginia Eaton Professor of Psychology at Stanford University**

Praise and words of appreciation have a significant impact on a leader's ability to motivate and inspire their teams. However, words can often be a double-edged sword as over-praising can make team members doubt the praiser's sincerity while criticism can seriously demotivate, even when it is given as constructive criticism. A successful leader provides team members with genuine feedback and appreciation in a way that helps them feel empowered, confident and self-reliant.

As a parent, it is easy to fall into the 'criticism trap' because we want our children to do better. Indeed, a significant part of the interaction we have with our children is based around negative comments, criticisms, judgements and observations that are often made unconsciously. But if we make too many negative comments, even if they are said with the best of intentions, we are inadvertently damaging our children's self-esteem.

Conversely, it is also easy to fall into the 'over-praising trap' because we want our children to be happy and feel good about themselves. If we over-praise, particularly with statements of 'evaluative praise' (such as "Good girl/boy", or "You're so smart"), this can lead them to become 'praise junkies' where they constantly seek approval and validation from others. It can even make them afraid of failure in the long-term.

This fear of failure can lead to children forming a 'Fixed Mindset', where they believe that intelligence and skills are innate rather than improved and grown through effort and practice. Children with a fixed mindset are less likely to take on new challenges as they are afraid of making a mistake and having their 'natural' talents called into question.

Kirstie (8) is having a conversation with her parents about her extra-curricular activities:

"I don't want to do ballet or piano anymore, it's boring." She tells them.

"But Kirstie, you used to enjoy piano and ballet so much, what's changed?"

"Nothing, I just don't want to do it anymore."

"But what about your piano recital, don't you want to show everyone how good you are? And how will you ever get to be a ballerina if you don't go to class?"

"But I'm not any good at piano, I'm nowhere near as good as the other girls, and I don't want everyone to laugh at me if I get it wrong. And ballet class is much too hard, so I've decided that I don't want to be a ballerina anymore." Kirstie replies and crosses her arms over her chest.

"You're such a natural when it comes to music and dance though Kirstie, you'd be wasting so much talent if you gave them up!"

Kirstie frowns in disbelief at her parents' words of encouragement and leaves without saying another word.

Research has shown that the way we speak to our children, and particularly the way we praise them, has a significant impact not only on their willingness to learn and to take on challenges in life, but subsequently on their self-esteem and their behaviour as a whole. This is because children naturally crave their parents' acceptance and appreciation so the way that we interact with them, including the nature of the comments that we make, directly influences the way they feel about themselves.

How to become a Leader parent

One of the key objectives as a parent is to develop a Growth Mindset in our children as this is the mindset that allows them to be curious about life, motivates them to want to learn and take on new challenges and makes them unafraid to make mistakes. To achieve this, research shows that it is important to let go of evaluative praise as it focuses on the child's 'innate' abilities and can make them afraid of failure, and instead acknowledge children for the effort that they have put into achieving something.

How to help develop a Growth Mindset and boost a child's confidence and self-esteem:

1. **Find things that they like and are good at**: Self-esteem comes from feeling good about ourselves and understanding what we're good at and ultimately what makes us unique. It's important that we allow kids to experiment with different activities so that they can find things they enjoy, because this will help them learn to enjoy the process and become less likely to give up in the face of difficulty. When children engage in a behaviour or activity purely for the enjoyment of it, they do so because it is intrinsically rewarding and not because they are trying to earn an external reward.

2. **Find things that will challenge them**: Self-esteem also comes from struggle and overcoming adversity. It's important that children don't only do things that come easily to them and that they find (age-appropriate) challenges that they can overcome. Encouraging children to find their own solutions to problems significantly increases their confi-

dence because it helps them to realise that they can overcome challenges without relying on another's intervention or praise. If they express frustration during a challenge and they say something along the lines of "I'm not good at this", we need to always remind them that they are not yet good at something. 'Yet' is a powerful word which is the epitome of a Growth Mindset vs. a fixed one, as it reminds children that this is a temporary state and they can improve things with effort.

3. **Celebrate mistakes:** To develop a Growth Mindset, children need to feel that mistakes are important as they can learn from them. One way to do this is to teach them that FAIL actually means 'First Attempt In Learning' and that taking action and failing would yield less regret than failing to try. Another way to do this is to share our mistakes (for example during meals or part of a regular **Family Meeting**) and ask children to share their own mistakes and what they have learnt from them. In Kirstie's example above, learning to celebrate mistakes would help her to see that mistakes are an essential part of the learning process and not something to be afraid of. This in itself can take away much of the pressure that many children feel to be 'perfect'.

4. **Praise the effort and the progress rather than the outcome:** For example, "I can see by your playing the piano how much you have practiced", or "You know your times tables by heart, I can see that you have put a lot of effort into learning these as you didn't know them as well last week". When we focus on a child's effort, rather than their achievements or level of ability, and we praise children only for the traits that they have the power to change, we encourage them to learn the art of motivation. We help them to recognise that sometimes tasks require us to put in effort over a long period of time and the importance of grit and perseverance. We want them to think, "Yes, I worked really hard to get to this result so it's worth making the effort in the future". In Kirstie's case, her parents' focus on her 'natural talent' are not helpful as she cannot change this, and they

should have focused instead on her effort and the progress she has made in her activities.

5. **Praise descriptively rather than using 'evaluative' praise:** We should focus on strategy and the process of learning rather than the outcome, and praise the steps a child takes as this shows them that each step is a necessary part of achieving something. Instead of saying, "Wow, this is so beautiful!" try asking your child a question, "How did you do this part?", or simply describe what we see, "Wow the chicken in your drawing looks so lifelike!". Children appreciate that interest in their work and how it was executed, and are more likely to realise their achievements and want to share them.

6. **Praise specific actions rather than their overall behaviour:** This allows children to realise that their behaviour is something that they *choose* rather than something they *are*. For example, instead of saying, "You behaved really well when Granny was here", say, "I really appreciated that you helped Granny get in and out of her chair during her visit". Also, 'staged' eavesdropping - for example praising your child to a partner or another adult within their hearing - can also be a great way to acknowledge a child's specific actions.

7. **Make it about them:** What we ultimately want is for children to develop their own power of self-evaluation, rather than become 'praise junkies', who are dependent on us to tell them if they are doing well. Instead of "I'm so proud of you", we can help them realise their own achievements by asking them instead, "You have worked hard and did well on this test, are you proud of yourself?", or "Are you happy with the result?", and once they answer, "Yes I am", we can always add: "I am proud of you too!".

8. **Be selective in your praise and be honest:** Praise everything children do and they will either discount what we are saying, or become dependent on praise for self-affirmation. So take care to not overdo it. Even young kids can see right through false praise, so it is important to remain honest.

However, some people have a tendency to 'under-praise' in fear that doing the opposite might spoil their child. This is not good either, as children do need encouragement and positive comments to feel good about what they do. If in doubt, just remember to follow the guidelines above for effective ways of encouraging them.

9. **Accentuate the positive, reduce the negative:** We need to make sure that our positives outweigh the negatives so that we fill a child's 'I'm capable' account instead of filling the 'I'm a failure' account. To do so, focus on their uniqueness rather than on their weaknesses. Research shows that children need at least three times more positive comments than negative ones. For example, rather than saying "No, that's not the way to do this", we suggest "I see that you've done it this way. There's another way of doing it that you might prefer, shall I show it to you?".

10. **Try not to criticise:** Even constructive criticism can be interpreted by children as being negative. Identify the good things in something that a child has done and ask them to explain the reason for their success (usually the effort that they've put into it). This helps fill the 'I'm capable account'. If we feel that there is room for improvement, then simply add: "Are you happy with the result" (as this allows children to tell us what they would like to improve) or "What could you better next time?".

Further examples for solving typical parenting challenges

For more ideas and some real-life stories on how to grow your child's self-esteem and resilience, you can download from Amazon our short eBook: *Raising Confident Kids - 10 Ways to Foster Self-Esteem & Avoid Typical Parenting Mistakes.*

✖ TOOL #21
Problem Solving

Objective: Empowering children to become critical thinkers and find solutions to their own problems

"Leaders think and talk about the solutions.
Followers think and talk about the problems."
Brian Tracy, Best-selling Author of
'The Psychology of Achievement'

"You teach me, I forget. You show me,
I remember. You involve me, I understand."
Edward O. Wilson, Author of
'The Meaning of Human Existence'

The most effective leaders know how to balance being directive and collaborative, and recognise the necessity and importance of both. Being collaborative and involving team members in problem-solving and decision-making empowers them and makes them feel motivated to deliver the results that they helped to define. Being collaborative with team members also shows them that they are valued as they feel that they 'have a say'.

As parents, we often skip straight to offering solutions to our children when they present us with a problem, or to implementing consequences or punishment when they make a mistake. This doesn't give them the opportunity to solve their own issues or to participate in finding solutions to improve their behaviour. In doing so, we are underestimating their ability to solve their own problems, and we are not empowering them to find solutions to these problems for themselves.

Mollie's about to pick her daughter up from school when she spots Sasha (8), standing with a group of girls at the gates. There are raised voices and Sasha looks upset, so Mollie decides to intervene:

"What's the problem girls? What's all the shouting about?" The girls quickly disperse, so Mollie puts her arm around her daughter's shoulders and walks her to the car.

"Are you okay, Sasha? What were those girls saying to you?"

"Nothing. It doesn't matter."

"Well, let me give you some advice, next time someone says something nasty to you, you should just walk away or go and tell a teacher. If that doesn't work, then the best thing you can do is stand up to them. Tell them that they're being immature and that you don't want to talk to them anymore – that's bound to work."

Sasha doesn't respond and stares at her shoes in silence.

"The least you could do is listen to me, Sasha. I'm trying to help you and all you can do is stare at your shoes!"

Sasha still doesn't respond and says very little else for the rest of the drive home.

When we choose to intervene because our child has encountered a problem of some kind, we are invariably doing it with the best of intentions. Unfortunately, rather than protecting our kids we are actually robbing them of an invaluable opportunity to find solutions for themselves. Seeing our children struggle with any kind of problem can be difficult, but when they learn to deal with it themselves, this encourages critical thinking and helps to increase their levels of resilience. So that when they encounter problems in the future, they will have confidence in their ability to cope.

How to become a Leader parent

Problem Solving becomes one of the most used tools of all our Toolkit once children are four or older because it is the most effective in empowering children to find solutions to the problems that they bring back home.

It is also the most effective at dealing with misbehaviour as it involves children in finding solutions to problems that occur in the wider family rather than focusing on consequences and punishment - which can have detrimental effects on motivation.

We can even involve children in setting rules, choosing logical consequences and by asking them how they would prefer to be reminded should a misbehaviour occur. This is a great way of teaching children to think for themselves and encourages them to be responsible for their own actions, which makes it far more effective than any other form of discipline.

It is much more motivating for children when we are as collaborative as we can possibly be and to involve them in decision-making and solution-finding wherever possible - but without forgetting that sometimes we need to be directive as ultimately, we remain their leader.

How to use Problem Solving:

This tool can be used in two different ways:

I. **Your child has a problem, which they want to share**: For example, they have no friends, or they don't like school or are struggling to do their homework on time (which by the way is *their* problem, not yours!):

1. **You should first actively listen to what your child has to say** without jumping in to offer solutions (refer to Tool #17 - **Emotion Coaching**).

2. **Then encourage your child to take ownership of their problem** by asking them, "**What could *YOU* do about this?**".

The answer to this question is usually, "I don't know", particularly if they've not been 'coached' to find solutions to their own problems before. So respond to this by saying, "Do you want me to help give you some ideas to start with?" or - particularly when they are younger: "Would you like me to tell you what other children have tried?":

3. If they say "No thank you", say "**Okay, but if you change your mind, I'm always here to listen.**"

4. **Give them different options of possible solutions**: If they say "Yes please", offer them at least two solutions. Younger children are quite likely to simply choose the first option suggested, so it's better to ensure that the first solution offered is one that they would be unlikely to choose. You could even use a joke idea to introduce a little humour into the problem-solving process (although make sure you clarify that it is a joke idea to avoid any confusion).

5. **Empower**: After explaining each solution, encourage them to evaluate by asking, "How would that work for you?". If no ideas arise simply say, "Let me have a think about it and check how other kids have dealt with this problem and I'll get back to you".

6. **Show interest, but avoid interfering**: Once a child has decided on which solution they think would be the most appropriate course of action (either one you've suggested or one they have come up with themselves), just say, "Let me know how it all works out - good luck!".

NB: If they haven't been inspired by any of the suggestions, then encourage them to keep working on it and refine their approach until they are able to come up with a solution for themselves.

The most important thing about this process is that it demonstrates a commitment to supporting and encouraging them to think for themselves, both now and in the future.

II. When you have a problem that you want to discuss with your child:

Let's say you would like your children to improve a certain aspect of their behaviour (for example, listening, being too slow in the morning, back-chatting, etc.). The most effective way to deal with these issues, particularly if they are recurring, it to involve your child in finding solutions to this issue when everyone is calmer, which can be several hours or days after the problem occurred:

1. Initiate a problem-solving session: You could start this while doing something that your child enjoys, or in the evening before reading a story or alternatively, incorporate this ses-

sion into a **Family Meeting** (see Tool #22). Identify exactly what the issue is without blaming the child for the behaviour, while explaining why this doesn't work for you.

For example, if a child has been rude, say, "When you spoke to me in that way, I felt hurt and disrespected." Keep it specific and do not combine several issues, as it would make it harder to find effective solutions.

2. **Ask your child questions that show that you're in it together:** "What could *WE* do about this?"

3. **Work together with your child to generate what possible solutions there may be to the problem in question**: Talk about what each of you could do differently next time the problem presents itself. For a child four or older, ask them to try to come up with their own suggestions before offering solutions so that they feel empowered.

4. **Listen to their suggestions carefully, asking them**: "And how do you think that would work for you?"

5. **Have a brainstorming session:** Discuss and decide on the best solutions and then brainstorm together about how to implement them.

6. **Ask your child how they would prefer to be reminded should they break an agreement**: If they don't have any ideas of their own, help them come up with a fun way to remind themselves. For example, you could use a funny phrase or a funny sound that will remind them of the problem-solving session, whenever they revert to the old misbehaviour. You could also suggest that you will tell them 'Rewind!' when they've done something that is not acceptable, so that they have the opportunity to do a 'do-over'. This is a fun and effective way to teach them to correct their attitude or behaviour without having to deliver a consequence.

7. **For children older than five, end with a discussion about logical consequences:** Discuss what the logical consequences should be in the event that they do not follow the agreement. This has the advantage of making them responsible for their own behaviour, and they are far less likely to

resist a consequence that they themselves have decided on, as they will feel that this is a 'fair' way of dealing with the situation.

Further examples for solving typical parenting challenges

1. Child refusing to cooperate

"When you refuse to do things that we agreed upon together, it doesn't give me much incentive to do things for you. What could *we* do to make sure this doesn't happen again?"

2. Child not listening or ignoring you

"When you appear to ignore me, I feel disrespected and upset. What could *we* do to make sure this doesn't happen again?"

3. Whining

"When you ask for something the way you did this morning, it makes it hard for me to listen to you. Whining doesn't work in this house, so what could *we* do to reduce the whining?"

4. Child constantly arguing and negotiating

"Don't you think arguing like we did yesterday prevents us both from doing lots of more enjoyable things together? What could *we* do to reduce the amount of time we spend arguing?"

5. Child refusing or making a fuss over homework

"You seem to be struggling to settle down to do the homework you have been given, do you have any thoughts as to how *you* might be able to make it easier to start work?". Remember that homework is their responsibility!

TOOL #22
Family Meetings

Objective: *To increase family harmony and foster empathy and understanding*

> *"Unity is strength . . . when there is teamwork and collaboration, wonderful things can be achieved."*
> **Mattie Stepanek, Best-Selling American Poet**

> *"If everyone is moving forward together, then success takes care of itself."*
> **Henry Ford, Founder of the Ford Motoring Company**

The most successful leaders recognise the importance of holding regular meetings, and how important they are for motivating and inspiring team members and ensuring that everyone is united in working towards a common goal. An effective leader will use this time to identify potential problems, so that the team can prevent and/or prepare for them and reduce any negative impact they may have upon team morale and productivity.

As a family, we may not always do this consciously, but we try to function as a team that shares similar goals and values, and that strives to be happy together. But as we are not a business, we tend not to have formal meetings and so have fewer 'real' and deep conversations about how we can achieve our family goals, what the needs of each family member are and what actions we are going to put in place to enable us to function together more effectively.

On the occasions when we do sit down to discuss something with our children, it's usually because we have a problem to talk about or an issue that needs raising. So if we rarely sit down with our children unless there's a problem, it's no surprise that they may be defensive or oppositional in such situations.

Jack has an important issue to discuss with the kids so he gets the family around the kitchen table:

"So kids, we have a very important issue that we need to discuss." *Jack begins.*

"Sounds like we're about to get told off", whispers Peter (14) to Kirstie (8).

"Stop whispering Peter, this is important so I need you to listen. Your Mum and I are sick and tired of tidying up after you all of the time, and have had enough of hearing you teasing and arguing with each other. You leave your toys and clothes all over the place, never do any of chores we set for you and you seem to expect your Mum and I to pick up after you all the time. We've had enough of it – you need to start helping out around the house and stop arguing with each other or there are going to be some serious consequences."

"But I took the rubbish out yesterday and no-one even had to ask me!" exclaims Peter. "It's Kirstie who never does anything to help out!" he says and points at his sister.

"That's not true at all, at least I keep my bedroom tidy – Peter's room is always messy and you and Mum never even tell him off for it!" says Kirstie, defending herself.

"See? This is exactly what we're talking about, off you go fighting with each other again."

"This is stupid, you haven't even said anything to Chloe (6) - just because she's the youngest, she gets away with everything!" Peter complains and pulls his phone out of his pocket, refusing to communicate any further, while the rest of the family continue to bicker around him.

The question is, how can we expect to function with a shared vision if we don't find time to sit down regularly as a family and discuss what is important to each family member, and particularly to us as parents? And how can we expect our children to be cooperative if we don't take the time to highlight the positive things that they are doing as well as the negative?

How to become a Leader parent

Just as team meetings are used in the workplace to ensure a unified and cohesive working environment, holding regular family meetings is key to building and maintaining a strong connection with our children and to redirecting any behaviour that we might disapprove of.

It's a way of making sure that all family members feel a sense of belonging and responsibility towards one another, and it provides an invaluable opportunity for each person to have their thoughts heard and their feelings acknowledged. This in itself is incredibly powerful as it helps to create a sense of family unity and togetherness and a sense of common purpose. They need not be too business-like, as you want the children to look forward to them, so try combining it with something pleasurable such as a family game.

Holding regular family meetings is a very effective way to increase our children's confidence and nurture their self-esteem. It provides the perfect forum in which to give encouragement and praise, and to discuss challenges and how to overcome them. As the meeting isn't a crisis meeting but a regular occurrence, the pressure if off and any challenges can be discussed in a non-heated and more helpful way.

It's important that we try to put a positive spin on any of the issues that we raise. If children feel as though they are being accused or singled out, then they will often take up a defensive position and become uncooperative. They may even try to shift blame by drawing attention to a sibling's behaviour as Peter and Kirstie do in the scenario above. But if we discuss issues in a positive way and talk about solutions rather than focusing on blame, this helps to unite the family and makes children more willing to address these issues as a team. It also helps to improve their behaviour as they are empowered by being able to participate in finding solutions to the family challenges.

How to hold Family Meetings:

1. Schedule in (ideally) one family meeting every week. During this meeting, everyone should sit together and switch

off their phones and other electronic devices. Children younger than four might not formally participate in the meeting as it is harder for them to have this kind of longer discussion. But they should ideally sit down next to the rest of the family and can occupy themselves by drawing or some other activity that will not disturb the meeting.

2. Elect two family members to act as Chairperson and Secretary.
   The role of the Chair is to lead the meeting to make sure that the agenda is covered and everyone gets to speak.

   The role of the Secretary is to take the meeting notes so that there is a record of decisions made during the meeting. Younger family members may need help with this.Although, this step may make it sound 'too serious', it provides a good structure and children will look forward to the day when they will be allowed to be Chair and/or Secretary (once they grow older and/or have more experience of participating in Family Meetings).

3. Open the meeting with compliments and gratitude. Each person should take a turn addressing every family member to express gratitude or give a compliment.

   Siblings will usually find difficult to express gratitude and give compliments to each other so we have to first model this behaviour ourselves - they will usually become more comfortable doing it after a few Family Meetings.

4. Ask every family member to share a moment that they have been proud of since the last meeting.

5. Go through the 'Agenda', which may include one or more of the following:

- Individual issues: each family member has the opportunity to raise their need or identify a problem they may be experiencing.

- Hold a **Problem Solving** (Tool #21) session to deal with family challenges.

- Decide on a chore system: allocate tasks and household duties. See **Family Contribution** - Tool #15.

- Plan activities and family fun days.

- At the end of the meeting, do something fun as a family that is age-appropriate (e.g. play a board game, or 'I went to the market and bought...').

- It may sound a bit cheesy, but it adds to the sense of bonding to end the meeting with a family hug!

Further examples for solving typical parenting challenges

1. Child refusing to cooperate, not listening, whining, arguing and negotiating, homework issues, etc.

See **Problem Solving** - Tool #21 for practical examples of how to address these challenges.

2. Child refusing to do chores/jobs

See **Family Contribution** - Tool #15 for practical examples of how to address this challenge.

3. Siblings fighting about toys and possessions

Bring the sharing issue at hand to a family meeting and problem solve together as to how your children could resolve their fights over possessions.

4. Siblings being violent or teasing

Family meetings can be used to initiate a problem-solving session (see **Problem Solving** - Tool #21), which allows each family member to offer their own ideas as to how the violence and teasing can be prevented in the future.

How to Fulfil Children's Potential

- Help your children develop a Growth Mindset - as opposed to a fixed mindset - by praising them for things that they have control over such as their effort and progress.

- Focus on your child's uniqueness by encouraging them to find things that they are good at.

- Find other things that are challenging for your children as this will help them develop their self-esteem and re-silience.

- Avoid falling into the common parenting traps of over-praising and using evaluative praise (e.g. "Good boy", "You're so smart") as children can become praise junkies and become afraid of failure, and they may start to doubt your sincerity.

- Empower children to think for themselves and to stand on their own two feet by encouraging them to find solutions to their own problems.

- Involve children in finding solutions to their mistakes so that you empower them to implement the improvements that they suggest. Remember to give them the opportunity to correct their mistakes with a gentle reminder, should a misbehaviour occur.

- Nurture the idea of family being a team and foster a spirit of unity and togetherness by holding regular family meet-ings where each family member can share gratitude and compliments and their needs, as this will allow for a much happier family life.

Your Notes

CONCLUSION

I sincerely hope that the ideas, insights and techniques described in this book and the parallels made with your knowledge and experiences from working life help to improve your confidence in your skills and ability as a parent. The parallels drawn between work and family life demonstrate that it is not necessary or useful to separate the two, and highlights just how much one aspect of our lives can influence another.

You have probably realised that most of the techniques in this book move away from the 'carrot and stick' approach, which is usually the default way that we parents get our kids to comply with our requests. As explained in Chapter 2, using the carrot, i.e. rewards, can backfire, decreasing a child's motivation to do things for themselves. What I hope I have shown in this book is how you can tap into the 'intrinsic motivation' children are born with to do things to the best of their ability.

The 'stick' is equally damaging because the connection and emotional bond that we have with our children should be the base of our influence - rather than the use of power - because it is this strong connection with us, and their willingness to keep this bond, that motivates them to behave 'appropriately'[32]. As in any organisation, the more the team feels that 'we're all in it together' and our interests and goals are aligned - and knowing that the leaders can lead us there - the better the outcome.

So the objective of many of the tools is to build a family environment of support and encouragement, and show our children that we share common goals and we need to help one another to reach them. The aim is also to empower children by being as collaborative as possible in the family decisions so that they feel that: 'If we all work together, and make a contribution for the sake of the greater good, we will all reach the common goals in a much more reasonable and efficient way.' However, as any good leader, we also need to be directive whenever needed as we are ultimately the decision maker and children need to understand the limits.

Some of the tools and techniques presented may have reaped immediate results for you while others may be more challenging to implement - it largely depends on your child's temperament and your own experience of applying the tools. Whatever your experience has been, it is crucial to remember that as in business, effective parenting is all about practice and requires consistency and this is what the 5-Week Programme that you will find in the next section can help you achieve.

For example, no one is born a public speaker and it takes time and practice to become really accomplished at it. The same is true of parenting. As we discovered in Chapter 1 with the concept of 'Outsight', change happens through action and the best way to become a Leader parent is through practice and repetition. So the most important thing is not to despair - we parents spend far too much time feeling guilty as it is!

As working parents, we will always be called upon to perform a balancing act between our lives at work and our lives at home. Through an understanding and ability to recognise the ways in which these two aspects of our lives relate to one another and overlap, work-life harmony can be achieved and have a transformative effect on our lives at home and in the workplace.

Remember to continually, yet subtly, review your expectations - of yourself and of your child. Because working parents tend to be more demanding of themselves, they also tend to be more demanding of their children. This can have a positive effect, as long as you keep in mind the importance of understanding your child and not allowing a healthy level of expectation to turn into an unrealistic one.

The impact that our choices as parents have on our children's lives cannot be emphasised enough. As parents, we are leading the next generation to fulfilling their potential and becoming active and responsible members of their community. Through an awareness and understanding of our role as leaders at home, we maximise the chances of our children adopting these same attributes and becoming successful leaders and parents of the future.

It is rewarding to realise that by making some changes to the decisions we make as parents, we make a positive difference to our own lives, to our children's and to the world as a whole. I fully believe that in this endeavour to raise children who are better prepared for the world, we are helping make the world become a better, more harmonious place for everyone.

We'd love to hear your family stories and parenting experiences, and we'll be happy to send you a free eBook as thanks. So please do get in touch by visiting **www.bestofparenting.com**.

You can subscribe to our free newsletter, download our free troubleshooting app, and find other material such as our online course to support you on every step of your parenting journey.

BONUS MATERIAL

Your 5-Week Programme to becoming a Leader parent

Working parents looking to make their family life stress-free and more enjoyable often ask for a programme for using the tools and techniques to allow them to reap the maximum benefit, given the small amount of time available to them.

If you stick to the suggested programme and are consistent in the application of the tools, you will see a significant reduction in the number of times your children react negatively or misbehave. More importantly, you will feel calmer and more confident in the face of misbehaviour and will have a better connection with your children.

To successfully complete the programme requires just 10 minutes of reading each day and around 30 minutes of practice. By practice, we mean the amount of time you spend with your children anyway, the only difference is that you'll be trying out the suggested tools.

To make our programme easier to use, we have created a simple structure that can be summarised as RAP: Read, Apply and Practice.

WEEK 1
Raising awareness and starting to improve the family dynamic

Read

The following 5 tools:
Understanding Your Strengths and Weaknesses (#1)
Teamwork (#2)
Understanding Your Children (#3)
Limited Choices (#6)
Presence (#16)

Apply

Apply the tools **Limited Choices** (#6) and **Presence** (#16) consistently throughout the first week and as often as you possibly can. You will be surprised by the amount of choices that you can actually give to your children!

If you have a partner, try to also use the tool **Teamwork (#2)**.

WEEK 1 NOTES

. . . .

. . . .

. . . .

. . . .

. . . .

. . . .

. . . .

WEEK 2

Preventing challenges and achieving family harmony

Read

> The following 5 tools:
> **Planning Ahead (#4)**
> **Creating Routines (#5)**
> **Asking Questions (#7)**
> **Positive Redirection (#9)**
> **Effective Communication (#10)**

Apply

Apply the tools **Planning Ahead (#4)**, **Asking Question (#7)** and **Positive Redirection (#9)** consistently throughout this second week.

Avoid the temptation to rush into using too many tools in one go. Our experience shows that it's better to apply one or two tools consistently every day to experience positive change rather than trying too many new things at the same time. The reason why we request that you read more tools than you should actually use each week is to enable you to be able to use the tools that best suit you, your child and your situation.

Practice - Stop, Start, Continue

Now that you have more awareness of your parenting style and you have started implementing some of the tools, you should have a better view of what is working with your child. To reinforce the positive change and ensure that it is long lasting, you can use the Stop, Start, Continue technique to help you prioritise the things that you want to focus on. The idea is to choose the following:

- 2 things you want to stop doing (e.g. nagging or getting angry)

- 2 things you want to start doing (e.g. using some of this week's new tools)

- 2 things that you want to continue doing (e.g. tools that already seem to be working for you).

Once you have decided on your 'Stop, Start, Continue' wish list, write them down somewhere you can easily refer to (Post-Its placed strategically around your home works well), and try to read them every morning so that you remain conscious of your intentions.

WEEK 2 NOTES

. . . .

. . . .

. . . .

. . . .

. . . .

WEEK 3
Setting clear boundaries and making children accountable for their actions

Read

The following 4 tools:
Positive & Enforceable Statements (#8)
Setting Rules/Clarifying Expectations (#11)
Mistakes as Opportunities for Learning (#18)
Logical and Delayed Consequences (#19)

Apply

Once you have read the tool **<u>Setting Rules/Clarifying Expectations (#11)</u>**, sit down with your partner (if you have one) and agree on House Rules and what is acceptable vs. unacceptable.

Apply the tools **Positive & Enforceable Statements (#8)** to replace all kinds of threats and apply consequences - rather than punishments - if your child misbehaves during this week (see Tool #19).

NB: Having reached this point, you may find that there are actually fewer opportunities to apply consequences - which is why this tool comes in week 3. At this stage you'll probably be experiencing far less misbehaviour from your children. This shift is likely to not only be due to the impact of your having successfully applied the tools, but also to you becoming more aware and more confident of your own parenting skills.

Practice - Stop, Start, Continue

Continue implementing the 2 things that you wanted to stop doing, 2 things that you want to start doing and 2 things that you want to do more of.

WEEK 3 NOTES

. . . .

. . . .

. . . .

. . . .

. . . .

. . . .

. . . .

. . . .

WEEK 4
Helping children to become responsible

Read

> The following 4 tools:
> **Leading by example (#12)**
> **Taking good care of Yourself (#13)**
> **Emotion Coaching (#17)**
> **Problem Solving (#21)**

Apply

Apply the tool **Emotion Coaching (#17)** consistently throughout the week and if your child is older than three, aim to hold a **Problem Solving (#21)** session to address a recurring challenge that you may have.

Practice - Stop, Start, Continue

Choose another set of 2 things that you want to stop doing, 2 things that you want to start doing and 2 things that you want to continue doing.

WEEK 4 NOTES

. . . .

. . . .

. . . .

. . . .

. . . .

. . . .

WEEK 5
Becoming a family team and preparing children for the future

Read

The following 4 tools:
Family Culture (#14)
Family Contribution (#15)
Growth Mindset (#20)
Family Meetings (#22)

Apply

Apply the tool **Growth Mindset (#20)** during this week. If one of your children is older than four, you should also aim to hold a **Family Meeting (#22)**, during which you can introduce the concept of **Family Culture (#14)** and the 2-minute quiz.

Practice - Stop, Start, Continue

Continue implementing the 2 things that you wanted to stop doing, 2 things that you want to start doing and 2 things that you want to continue doing.

WEEK 5 NOTES

. . . .

. . . .

. . . .

. . . .

. . . .

. . . .

WEEK 6 and beyond

By this stage in the programme, you should be experiencing a marked improvement in your family's dynamics and in your children's behaviour. Hopefully, rather than relying on punishment and 'consequences' to enforce good behaviour, you will be focusing on the more positive 'virtuous' cycle provided by an improved connection with your child and the use of problem-solving techniques. The benefits of such a shift should include being able to prevent many troublesome issues from occurring in the first place and quickly finding solutions to challenges and problems when they do occur.

Practice - Stop, Start, Continue

However, since it is easy to fall back into old habits it is essential to keep practising each of the tools that you have found most useful until they start to come more naturally.

During these 5 weeks, you will have probably focused on the tools that you have found useful and relatively easy to implement - such as **Limited Choices (#6)** or **Asking Questions (#7)**, as these are usually parents' favourites.

You are now in a good position to start **gradually** introducing other tools into your daily life. Each week, simply pick a few new tools that seem most appropriate to your situation, and apply them, alongside the tools that you have already mastered.

Since most tools are applicable to children of all ages, they will continue to be useful throughout your child's progress into adulthood. So keep returning to your Toolbox for assistance and reminders throughout your parenting journey. For example, if you are a parent with children of toddler age, you will find that some tools (for e.g. **Family Culture #14**, **Problem Solving #21**, etc.) will only become really effective once your children start being able to use reason and can find solutions to problems.

Finally, keep in mind that **Family Meetings #22** are a great way to keep introducing and applying many of the tools in your Toolbox (for e.g. **Family Contribution #15, Emotion Coaching #17, Problem Solving #21**, etc.). So, if your kids are 4 years and older, we highly recommend that you start regularly scheduling these.

We'd love to know if this programme has worked for you! Contact us at **contact@bestofparenting.com** to let us know and we will send you a free eBook to thank you.

If you feel the need for a bit more help, we are always here to support you in your parenting journey. You can refer to our website **www.bestofparenting.com** to download our free app or to join our online parenting courses or a private coaching session.

Programme for other carers

As working parents, you may have several other people involved in your child's education such as relatives, childminders, nannies, etc., particularly if you're both working or if you're a single parent.

This Toolbox is equally invaluable and effective for carers. You may have noticed that some carers are sometimes more effective than us parents in dealing with our children? That's generally because emotions - such as anger or fear - often get in the way of the effectiveness of some of the tools, and carers usually have the advantage of having more 'emotional distance' than parents.

However, there is a slight variation in the type of tools that we recommend to carers, because of the difference in their relationship with the children in their care. For example, we would recommend that carers implement **Delayed Consequences** (Tool #19) as opposed to Logical/Immediate Consequences, because it will allow them to consult with parents as to the most appropriate consequence for a child's misbehaviour. This strategy enables both parents and carers to be more aligned in their thinking, and allows the child to feel the consistency in the new methods used.

Just as with parents, it's important that carers avoid the temptation to rush into using too many tools in one go.

It is better to apply just a handful of tools consistently every week to experience positive change, as children need a time of adaptation.

What follows is a 'mini-programme' for carers' that just contains the tools that are most useful and relevant for carers.

WEEK 1

Read and Apply

Planning Ahead (#4)

Creating Routines (#5):

NB: carers can implement this tool only if you have already created a routine with your children

Limited Choices (#6)

Asking Questions (#7)

WEEK 2

Read and Apply

Positive and Enforceable Statements (#8)

Positive Redirection (#9)

Effective Communication (#10)

Emotion Coaching (#17)

WEEK 3

Read and Apply

Setting Rules and Clarifying Expectations (#11)

NB: You should agree with carers which rules you want to be enforcing

Mistakes as Opportunities for Learning (#18)

NB: you should agree with carers what mistakes are afford-able, i.e. that you're comfortable that they let your children make while you're not around.

Logical and Delayed Consequences (#19)

NB: Carers would ideally be applying delayed consequences and checking with you what the most appropriate conse-quences are for our children's actions. You could also decide with them on a few 'standard' logical consequences for typical behaviour.

Trouble-shooting top 20 parenting challenges

1. Refusing to cooperate

One of the most common challenges for working parents who are often pressed for time is when our children refuse to cooperate with us, particularly when we are tired or stressed. The following tools are designed to help you reduce power struggles, avoid unnecessary conflict with your children and increase their levels of cooperation:

Quick and easy solutions: 5 minutes max

ॐ Tool #6 – Limited Choices
"Do you want to do this now or in a couple of minutes?"

ॐ Tool #7 – Asking Questions
"How do we do this in this house?"

ॐ Tool #8 – Positive & Enforceable Statements
"I take children to the park (or wherever they want to go) who have done … (whatever you want them to do)."
Or: "Children who want to eat dessert need to finish their lunch."

ॐ Tool #11 – Setting Rules/Clarifying Expectations
"This is the new rule: in this house, children have to tidy their room by the end of each day."

Solutions requiring a little more time or practice

ॐ Tool #19 – Logical & Delayed Consequences

"Sadly, since you haven't tidied your room, you are going to have to stay and tidy it now rather than going to the park."

Or delayed: "You remember how I said I would keep the toys I picked up if you didn't tidy your room? Well, it's such a shame, but I had to pick them up." (and you can keep the toys for a few days).

ᔕ Tool #21 – Problem Solving (age 3+)
"When you refuse to do things that we agreed upon together, it doesn't give me much incentive to do things for you. What could we do to make sure this doesn't happen again?"

2. Not listening/Ignoring you

Asking our child to do something over and over again is frustrating for even the most patient of parents, yet it is one of the most common problems that parents face. It is very normal for children to ignore us for the reasons set out in the tool **Understanding Your Children** (#3). However, if we are trying to keep to a busy work schedule, it can be difficult to 'keep our cool' when our child is wasting time that we don't have. Rather than lose your temper (or your sanity!), you can deal with the situation more effectively by applying these tools:

Quick and easy solutions: 5 minutes max

ᔕ Tool #6 – Limited Choices
"Would you rather do this now, or after you've finished your drawing?"

ᔕ Tool #7 – Asking Questions
"What are you supposed to do now?" or "What do we do in this house after breakfast?"

ᔕ Tool #8 – Positive & Enforceable Statements
"I listen to children who listen to me".

Tool #10 – Effective Communication
The most effective way to increase your chances of being listened to is to get close to your child and get down to their level to speak to them. You can also try whispering; it is usually very effective.

ᔕ Tool #11 – Setting Rules/Clarifying Expectations
"This is the new rule: in this house, we do things for children who listen to us."

Solutions requiring a little more time or practice

❧ Tool #19 – Logical & Delayed Consequences
"Sadly, because you have chosen not to listen to me, I'm not going to be able to play with you right now."
Or delayed: "Sadly, because you chose not to listen to me earlier on, we now won't be able to go and get an ice cream."
Or: "I am not feeling listened to and that is draining my energy, and so I no longer have enough energy to take you to the park."

❧ Tool #21 – Problem Solving (age 3+)
"When you appear to ignore me, I feel disrespected and upset. What could *we* do to make sure this doesn't happen again?"

---

3. Whining

Children will often use whining as a way of trying to get what they want, and although we shouldn't give in or react to this, this is often far easier said than done. Work commitments might mean that we don't get to spend as much time with our children as we would like, so we may find ourselves overcompensating by giving our children what they ask for even though we shouldn't be giving in to some of their 'wants'. Conversely, we may be feeling so tired from work that we allow ourselves to become 'triggered' by our child's whining and end up shouting at them to stop. Rather than allowing ourselves to get caught up in a vicious cycle, we can choose to apply one of the following tools instead:

Quick and easy solutions: 5 minutes max

❧ Tool #7 – Asking Questions
"Do you think that I can understand you when you speak this way?"

❧ Tool #8 – Positive & Enforceable Statements
"I listen to children who speak in the same tone of voice as mine."

❧ Tool #9 – Positive Redirection

"You can have a chocolate bar later, but you can have an apple right now."

◈ Tool #11 – Setting Rules/Clarifying Expectations
"This is the new rule: in this house, children who whine don't get what they are asking for."

◈ Tool #17 – Emotion Coaching
"I hear that you want an ice-cream and you can have one after dinner", and then you can repeat "I heard you" or "I know" in a calm tone of voice until the whining stops and without giving in. This is the most effective tool to diffuse whining as long as you are consistent.

Solutions requiring a little more time or practice

◈ Tool #19 – Logical & Delayed Consequences
"I know that you want an ice cream, but sadly the rule in this house is that children who whine cannot get what they are asking for."

Or delayed: "All this whining is causing me an energy drain, I'll need your help getting some energy back."

◈ Tool #21 – Problem-Solving (age 3+)
"When you ask for something the way you did this morning, it makes it hard for me to listen to you. Whining doesn't work in this house, so what could *we* do to reduce the whining?"

4. Arguing and negotiating

After a busy day of dealing with office politics, no parent wants to come home and have to deal with yet more conflict in the form of an argumentative child. Although we may be tempted to either negotiate with them or assert our authority in order to try to resolve the conflict, we can avoid becoming caught up in a 'battle of wills' with our child by applying one or more of the following tools:

Quick and easy solutions: 5 minutes max

၆ Tool #6 – Limited Choices
"Do you want to leave the park now or in five minutes?"

၆ Tool #7 – Asking Questions
"Do you think that I can understand you when you speak this way?"

၆ Tool #9 – Positive Redirection
"Sure we can go to the park once you have finished your homework" instead of "No you can't go to the park, and you know perfectly why: you still haven't done your homework!"

၆ Tool #17 – Emotion Coaching
"I hear that you would like to go to your friend's place and you can do this after finishing your homework". And if they start arguing and negotiating, you can repeat "I heard you" or "I know" in a calm tone of voice without giving in, until they stop arguing.

Solutions requiring a little more time or practice

၆ Tool #19 – Logical & Delayed Consequences
"As you know, in this house, those who argue when Mummy has made a clear decision get less than what they were asking for in the first place, so we now have to leave your friend's house earlier."
Or delayed: "Sadly, when you started arguing with me in the shop last time we were buying you clothes, it doesn't give me much incentive to go shopping with you, so I will go shopping alone today, but there will be other opportunities to go shopping together."
Or delayed: "All this arguing really gives me an energy drain, how are you going to put energy back into Mummy?"

၆ Tool #21 – Problem-Solving (age 3+)
"Don't you think arguing like this prevents us both from doing lots of more enjoyable things together? What could *we* do to reduce the amount of time we spend arguing?"

5. Refusing or making a fuss over homework

After a busy day at the office, the last thing any parent wants is to come home and have to deal with a child who causes a fuss or refuses to complete their homework. It's at times like this, when we may be stressed and tired from working all day, that we are most likely to find ourselves reacting to such situations by shouting or losing our temper. Raising our voice or getting angry can make the issue worse as it can cause our children to go into fight, flight or freeze mode and this makes it more difficult for them to think rationally (see Tool #3 - **Understanding Your Children**). To avoid this, you can diffuse the situation and prevent it from escalating by applying the following tools:

Quick and easy solutions: 5 minutes max

ॐ Tool #6 – Limited Choices
"Would you like to do your homework now or after playing a little game with me?".

Or "Would you like to do your homework sitting beside me or up in your own room?"

ॐ Tool #7 – Asking Questions
"What are you supposed to do now (or before watching TV), …?"

ॐ Tool #8 – Positive & Enforceable Statements
"I will take children who have finished their homework to their friend's house."
Or: "Sure, I'll be able to help you with your homework, once you have made a head start."

Tool #11 – Setting Rules/Clarifying Expectations
"In this family, we complete our work before we play."

Solutions requiring a little more time or practice

֍ Tool #17 – Emotion Coaching
"There seems to be something that's worrying you about your homework this week. Would you like to have a chat about it before you start working?"

Tool #19 – Logical & Delayed Consequences
"Sadly, you haven't done your homework yet, which means that you won't be able to watch TV."
Or delayed: "Sadly, last night you chose not to respect the 'do your homework' rule – that you had previously committed to – so we won't be able to go to the cinema tonight."
Or: "All this hassle around homework is giving me an energy drain. How are you going to work at giving me back energy?"

Tool #21 – Problem-Solving (age 3+)
"You seem to be struggling to settle down to do the homework you have been given, do you have any thoughts as to how *you* might be able to make it easier to start work?". Remember that homework is their responsibility!

---

6. Morning issues: Taking too long to do everything

Morning time tends to be one of the most challenging times of the day for working parents. When you're trying to stick to a schedule and you need to get you and the kids to work and school on time and your child is taking too long to get their shoes on etc. this can be somewhat frustrating to say the very least! When your children are wasting time that you don't have to spare, this can cause you to be late for work and end up negatively impacting upon your whole day. To avoid this from happening, you can save yourself up to an hour each day by simply applying one or more of our tools that have been adapted specifically for time-poor, working parents.

Quick and easy solutions: 5 minutes max

∽ Tool #4 – Planning Ahead
Think of the things that you can prepare in advance, for example, give them **Limited Choices** (see below) of what they would like to wear the next day the night before. You can also wake them up a bit earlier!

∽ Tool #6 – Limited Choices
"Would you rather use the 30 minutes that you have until breakfast to get dressed, or use just ten minutes for dressing and use the remaining 20 minutes to play a fun game with me?"

∽ Tool #7 – Asking Questions
Once you've created a routine (see below), you can ask your child: "What are you supposed to do next?"

∽ Tool #8 – Positive & Enforceable Statements
"My car leaves in five minutes and I take children to school dressed or not dressed." This works better if you take children to school by car as you need to follow through. If they are not dressed on time, you should take the remaining clothes in a bag: they will usually get dressed in the car before arriving at school and they are much more likely to get dressed on time the next day!

∽ Tool #11 – Setting Rules/Clarifying Expectations
"This is the new rule: in this house, children have to get dressed before breakfast."

Solutions requiring a little more time or practice

∽ Tool #5 – Creating Routines
Work out a routine *with* your child that describes, and even illustrates, each of the morning activities and let this routine become 'the boss'.

∽ Tool #19 – Logical & Delayed Consequences
"It's such a shame, as you've taken so long to get dressed, you're not going to have time to have your favourite breakfast as it would take too long".

ళ Tool #21 – Problem-Solving (age 3+)
"I feel frustrated when you don't get ready in time because it makes us late for school and I also arrive late at work. What could *we* do next time to help you get ready faster? Do you want ideas of what other children have tried?"

7. Bedtime challenges: Not wanting to go to bed or sleep

For busy working parents whose time is limited, a child who refuses to go to bed or sleep at night can present a real problem. Children become irritable and disagreeable when they don't get enough sleep (as do parents!), so the problems aren't just limited to bedtime, as day time also becomes more of a challenge as a result. With issues such as these, planning is prevention, so apply one or more of the following tools so that you can avoid such problems from occurring in the first place and deal with them more effectively when they do:

Quick and easy solutions: 5 minutes max

ళ Tool #6 – Limited Choices
"Would you like to go to bed now or in ten minutes?"
Or "Would you like me to help you up to bed or would you like to go on your own?"

ళ Tool #7 – Asking Questions
Once you've created a routine (see below), you can ask your child: "What are you supposed to do next?"

ళ Tool #8 – Positive & Enforceable Statements
"I read a story in 5 minutes to children who are in pyjamas and who have brushed their teeth."

ళ Tool #11 – Setting Rules/Clarifying Expectations
"The new rule is: 'grown up's time begins at 8pm, which means that children need to remain in their room, even if they decide not to go to sleep immediately."

Solutions requiring a little more time or practice

✎ Tool #5 – Creating Routines
Devise a 'going to sleep' ritual *with* your child that describes, and even illustrates, each of the evening activities (a prayer, poem or lullaby often helps calm a child).

✎ Tool #19 – Logical & Delayed Consequences
"Sadly, since you are choosing not to get into bed on time, I am going to have to read you a shorter story tonight."
Or delayed: "It's really sad, but since you wouldn't stay in bed the other night, you need to go to bed earlier tonight so I can't allow you to watch TV."
Or: "All this dithering about is causing me an energy drain, I'll need your help getting some energy back."

✎ Tool #21 – Problem-Solving (age 3+)
"It makes me frustrated when you won't get into bed at the right time because it means that the next day you are tired, less able to concentrate and moody. What do you think *we* could do about this?"

---

8. Hooked on screen, TV, iPads and other electronic devices

Many of us rely on our smartphones and tablets for work; we frequently have to check email, take work phone calls, etc., which can make it difficult to tell our children to cut their screen-time down at times when we feel that they are becoming overly reliant on them. However, research shows that screens are addictive and it is important for children to spend time playing and doing other activities, and particularly spend time outside the house. So it is essential to set clear boundaries so that children do not spend too much time on screens. We can deal with the situation far more effectively and reduce its negative impact with these key tools:

Quick and easy solutions: 5 minutes max

✎ Tool #6 – Limited Choices

"Do you want to play with the iPad for 30 minutes now or after you have finished your homework?"

Or choose alternative activities to do together (if you have time!), e.g. "Would you rather we look at old photos and do a collage of the last year or make cookies with me?"

✎ Tool #7 – Asking Questions
"What is our house rule regarding screens?"

✎ Tool #8 – Positive & Enforceable Statements
"Children who want to use the iPad/play an electronic game need to have finished their homework".

✎ Tool #11 – Setting Rules/Clarifying Expectations
"The rule in this house is that children can spend 30 minutes on screens every day - you can choose between TV and iPad." You could even create a system of 'vouchers' with a certain amount of time printed on them (e.g. 30 minutes of the iPad) that are then distributed fairly amongst your children on a weekly basis. So each child would get a number of these vouchers per week, and if they finish them, they have to wait for the following week to use screens. This makes them more responsible for time allocation.

✎ Tool #17 – Emotion Coaching
"I hear that you would really like to play on your tablet, and you can do this after finishing your homework". And if they start arguing and negotiating, you can repeat "I heard you" or "I know" in a calm tone of voice without giving in, until they stop arguing.

Solutions requiring a little more time or practice

✎ Tool #12 – Leading by Example
Restricting your screen time and trying not to check your phone in front of your kids too often is a great example that you can set for your children.

✎ Tool #19 – Logical & Delayed Consequences
"Sadly since you chose to break the rule about agreeing to leave

the screen when asked, I am now going to have to take it away for a couple of days."

Or delayed: "Since you refused to get off the screen when we were at Grandad's, you're not going to be able to play any electronic game today."

Or: "When you choose to watch a series on my iPad without asking permission, this gives me an energy drain, and I'm going to have to do something about it but not now."

✎ Tool #21 – Problem-Solving (age 3+)
"When you appear to ignore my requests to stop using the iPad, I feel disrespected and upset. You seem to be having trouble staying away from the screens? What could we do about this?"

9. Tantrums

Trying to cope with a child who is having a tantrum can be difficult at the best of times. But when we have had a busy day at work and are in desperate need of some rest and relaxation, trying to stay calm and composed in the face of a tantruming child proves to be even more of a challenge. Keep in mind that tantrums are normal and that it's how you deal with them that will directly impact how long they last and their frequency. Rather than losing your temper and allowing things to escalate, you can prevent them and diffuse the situation by using one or more of these effective tools:

For more ideas on how to deal with Tantrums, you can also download on Amazon our short eBook: **Tantrums: A step-by-step guide to preventing and diffusing your child's outbursts.**

Quick and easy solutions: 5 minutes max

✎ Tool #4 – Planning Ahead
Primary causes of tantrums are tiredness, hunger, lack of activity, or sudden changes in environment so make sure that you have addressed your kids' basic needs first.

❧ Tool #6 – Limited Choices

"I am hearing that you really want to eat ice cream, would you like to eat it after dinner or tomorrow after lunch?"

Or "I can see you really want this toy, would you like to put it on your birthday wish list or on your list for Santa?"

❧ Tool #7 – Asking Questions

"Is there anything I can do to help?"

❧ Tool #9 – Positive Redirection

"Sure, you can have this sweet at snack time." Instead of "No! You can't have this sweet as you haven't had lunch yet".

❧ Tool #17 – Emotion Coaching

Do not discount your child's feeling. Connect with them, name their feelings (for e.g. "I can see you are very upset…") and help them redirect their emotion.

Solutions requiring a little more time or practice

❧ Tool #16 – Presence (Aka One-on-one Time)

Giving your child some special time regularly is a great way to prevent tantrums from happening.

❧ Tool #21 – Problem-Solving (age 3+)

"When you throw yourself on the floor because you want something, it doesn't make me want to give it to you, what do you think would be a better way to ask me for something?"

---

10. Siblings fighting about toys and physical possessions

It can be difficult to resist the urge to play peacemaker and/or referee when our children are involved in fights and squabbles over toys and possessions. Time is precious for working parents, and nobody wants to spend the free time that they do have watching their children fight with one another. However, it's important to take a step back and let them learn how to deal with, and ultimately resolve, the conflict for themselves. Next time your children have an argument or disagreement, try not to intervene immediately and implement one of the following tools instead:

Quick and easy solutions: 5 minutes max

୨୬ Tool #7 – Asking Questions
"What is our house rule regarding toys and sharing?"

୨୬ Tool #11 – Setting Rules/Clarifying Expectations
It's useful to set 'property rights' to avoid sibling fights over toys and possessions and possibly create 'special/sacred shelves' for each child. This type of house rule is an effective way of clarifying what possession can be shared, when and with whom.
e.g. "In this house, toys that are not kept on your special shelves can be shared."

୨୬ Tool #17 – Emotion Coaching
"I can see that you are upset by what your brother did. I trust that you will be able to resolve this with him."

Solutions requiring a little more time or practice

୨୬ Tool #19 – Logical & Delayed Consequences
"This is so sad, I see that you don't seem to be able to play with this toy without fighting, so unfortunately I'm going to have to take it away for a while."
Or delayed: "Sadly, after all the fighting between you and your sister this morning over that game meant that I had no choice but to take it away."
Or: "All this fighting is giving me an energy drain and you're going to have to put back energy into Daddy if you'd like me to take you to the park."

୨୬ Tool #21 – Problem-Solving (age 3+)
"You seem to be fighting over possessions a lot, what do you think would make you most willing to share your toys with each other?"

꙲ Tool #22 – Family Meeting (age 4+)
Bring the sharing issue at hand to a family meeting and problem solve all together as to how siblings could resolve their fights over possessions. This allows everyone to express their needs and to find that the process is 'fair', so they are empowered and much more likely to comply.

11. Siblings using violence and teasing

When we see our children fighting and teasing one another it is very tempting to try to intervene in the hope of restoring the peace. Unfortunately, this often serves only to make the situation worse. Instead of trying to resolve the conflict for them, it's much more effective to be an interested rather than an active observer, and we can do this by implementing these key tools:

Quick and easy solutions: 5 minutes max

꙲ Tool #7 – Asking Questions
"What is our house rule regarding fighting?"

꙲ Tool #11 – Setting Rules/Clarifying Expectations
"The new rule is: fighting/teasing is unacceptable in this house."

Solutions requiring a little more time or practice

꙲ Tool #16 – Presence (Aka One-on-one Time)
A great way to reduce any type of sibling rivalry is to give each of your children some special time, one-to-one.

꙲ Tool #19 – Logical & Delayed Consequences
"Hitting is not ok, it seems like you both need some Time-Away in separate rooms to calm down".
Or delayed: "It's quite sad, but given how you were fighting earlier, this behaviour drained me of my energy, so now I don't have the energy to take you to your friend's house."

꙲ Tool #21 – Problem-Solving (age 3+)
"I can see that you felt angry enough to hit your sister, but you need to know that violence is not ok – it upsets everyone and

doesn't solve anything. What can we do so that it doesn't happen again?"

∿ Tool #22 – Family Meeting (age 4+)
The above problem-solving session is best done in the context of a family meeting, where every family member can give their own ideas as to how the violence and teasing can be prevented in the future.

12. Shopping struggles

Trying to get the shopping done when you have your children with you and are pushed for time can prove to be a stressful experience for any parent. You may be trying to pick up something for dinner after a challenging day at work, and all you want to do is get home so that you can relax and unwind. But when your children are constantly asking you to buy them treats and refusing to cooperate, a simple trip to the shops can end up being more exhausting than a busy day at the office! Thankfully, we can avoid the stress of shopping with children with these simple, yet highly effective tools:

Quick and easy solutions: 5 minutes max

∿ Tool #4 – Planning Ahead
Before the shopping trip, agree with your child what the rules are e.g. - if you're willing to buy them something: "I am willing to buy you one sweet, toy or magazine that costs less than £3."

∿ Tool #7 – Asking Questions
"What did we agree before going to the supermarket?"

∿ Tool #8 – Positive & Enforceable Statements
"We will take children shopping who don't constantly ask us to buy them things."
Or "I buy things for children who ask me without whining and who are capable of respecting me when I say 'No'."

∿ Tool #9 – Positive Redirection
"Sure you can buy it, as long as you can pay it with your pocket money" (for children who receive a weekly allowance).

Or "Would you rather add it to your birthday or Christmas wish list?"

✎ Tool #11 – Setting Rules/Clarifying Expectations
"This is the rule: children who want to come to the supermarket cannot whine or argue and ask for things."

Solutions requiring a little more time or practice

✎ Tool #19 – Logical & Delayed Consequences
"It's really sad, but since you are not following our agreement, we will have to put back the nice stuff we found and leave the shop." This might be difficult if you live far away, but remember that implementing this consequence means that it will be much less likely to happen again. Otherwise, you can implement a delayed consequence instead.
Or delayed: "I'd love to take you to the supermarket, but unfortunately, given how you behaved last time *(try to be more specific if you can)*, I'm not going to be able to."

✎ Tool #21 – Problem-Solving (age 3+)
"I'm sure you don't like it when your sister begs you repeatedly for something and then throws a scene. Well I don't like it when you do it either. What would be a better way of dealing with this when we're at the supermarket?"

---

13. Negative attitude

Working parents often feel guilty about not getting to spend as much time with their children as they'd like, so when we do get to spend time with them we want to make sure that it truly 'counts'. But if our children are exhibiting a negative attitude, spending quality time with them isn't as easy or as pleasant as we might hope. A negative attitude can make us feel as though our children are being ungrateful, when we are working so hard to give them everything they need. To diffuse the situation and stop yourself from trying to change their attitude or adding to the negativity, try applying one or more of the following tools instead:

Quick and easy solutions: 5 minutes max

༄ Tool #6 – Limited Choices
The more your fulfil your child's need for control and autonomy with **Limited Choices**, the less negative they will be so give these as often as possible.

༄ Tool #7 – Asking Questions
"Given your attitude, do you think that I'm going to want to continue playing with you?"

༄ Tool #8 – Positive & Enforceable Statements
"I do things for children who show a positive attitude."

Solutions requiring a little more time or practice

༄ Tool #16 – Presence (Aka One-on-one Time)

Spending some special time with your child is one of the best ways to reduce their overall negativity.

༄ Tool #17 – Emotion Coaching
"You seem to be a bit down today and you sound a bit negative, would you like to tell me how that feels for you right now?"

༄ Tool #20 – Growth Mindset
Research shows that 80% of parents' interaction with their children is based around negative comments and criticism. To reduce negativity and increase children's positivity, use the 10 steps to developing a Growth Mindset.

༄ Tool #21 – Problem-Solving (age 3+)
For example, "When you react negatively to something that I did for you I feel really frustrated, and it doesn't encourage me to continue making efforts for you. What could *we* do to make sure that this doesn't happen?"

14. Back-chatting, being rude and swearing at you or other people

When our children are rude to us or other people, it can make us feel as though we are failing in our role as parents. We may feel so ashamed or embarrassed by their behaviour that we end up over-reacting to the situation and making it even worse. What we have to remember is although this type of behaviour is unpleasant, it's also perfectly natural (did you know that seven is often labelled 'the age of rudeness'?) and is not an indication of a permanent attitude problem. This doesn't mean that we should just ignore it however, but we can choose to deal with this issue in a constructive rather than an inflammatory way with these tools:

Quick and easy solutions: 5 minutes max

☙ Tool #7 – Asking Questions
"Is this the way we speak to each other in this house?"
Or "Do you think I am going to want to give you what you've just asked for now that you've used this tone of voice?"

☙ Tool #8 – Positive & Enforceable Statements
"In this family we listen to people who speak to each other properly."
Or: "I give my attention to children who are polite".

☙ Tool #12 – Leading by Example
We need to be aware of whether our children are just copying our behaviour, and to make sure we don't use 'rude' words with them or with others.

☙ Tool #11 – Setting Rules/Clarifying Expectations
"In this family we try very hard not to swear" (as this applies to you too!)

Solutions requiring a little more time or practice

☙ Tool #19 – Logical & Delayed Consequences

"This rudeness is draining me of energy, I am going to need your help restoring my energy levels, as otherwise I won't be able to take you to your friend's house".

Or delayed "It's a shame that you still think it is ok to be rude to me, I won't do something about it now, but I will do about this at a later date."

֍ Tool #21 – Problem-Solving (age 3+)

"When you asked me for this earlier in that rude voice, it really didn't give me any incentive to give it to you. What do you think would have been a better way to achieve what you wanted?"

---

15. Being bossy

The last thing that any parent wants is come home and have to deal with a bossy child! Our instinct may be to assert our authority, or we may find their behaviour amusing or we may simply be too tired to deal with it at all. The best way to deal with the situation however, is by staying calm, taking a deep breath and following these step-by-step tools:

Quick and easy solutions: 5 minutes max

֍ Tool #6 – Limited Choices

"Do you want to get up now or in five minutes?". Replacing as many of our commands as possible with Limited Choices is the best way to reduce bossiness as it fulfils our child's need for control.

֍ Tool #7 – Asking Questions

"Do you think asking this way is going to get you what you want?"

Or "It sounds like you want me to do something for you, can you think of a better way of asking for it?"

֍ Tool #8 – Positive & Enforceable Statements

"I listen to children who talk to me in a different tone of voice."

❧ Tool #11 – Setting Rules/Clarifying Expectations
"This is the new rule: in this house, we do things for children who know how to ask respectfully."

Solutions requiring a little more time or practice

❧ Tool #5 – Creating Routines
With the help of your child, create a routine around regular tasks, this will enables the routines to 'be the boss' and reduce the orders/commands in the household.

❧ Tool #12 – Leading by Example
It is natural for our children to reproduce what they see and hear. Be aware of this and try and reduce your own 'bossiness'.

❧ Tool #19 – Logical & Delayed Consequences
"It's a shame, given how you just spoke to me, I'm not going to be able to take you to your friend's house."
Or delayed: "Sadly, because of the way you tried to order me around last night I now don't feel like going for a bike ride with you."
Or "All this bossiness is giving me an energy drain."

❧ Tool #21 – Problem-Solving (age 3+)
"When you are this bossy to me, I don't feel like listening to you and no one will around you, what do you suggest would be a better solution?"

16. Feeling insecure or lacking confidence

It's only natural that as parents, we want to see our children thrive, so it can make us feel us if we have failed in some way when our child is feeling insecure or lacking confidence in their ability. As working parents, we know only too well the challenges that children will face during their working lives. So when we see our child is struggling in some way, many parents start to worry about their child's ability to cope with the 'real world'. Rather than overreacting by 'swooping in' and trying to rescue our children from their distress, we can deal with the situation far more effectively with these step-by-step tools:

For more ideas on how to grow your child's confidence and self-esteem, you can download from Amazon our short eBook: ***Raising Confident Kids - 10 Ways to Foster Self-Esteem & Avoid Typical Parenting Mistakes.***

Quick and easy solutions: 5 minutes max

❧ Tool #6 – Limited Choices
A child who feels insecure probably feels disempowered. So what better way to make them feel confident and in control than by asking them to make as many (limited) choices as possible?

❧ Tool #7 – Asking Questions
"Is there anything that I can do to help you with this?"

❧ Tool #9 – Positive Redirection
Try to limit the amount of times that you use the word 'No' and replace it with more positive sentences. This will increase your child's motivation.

❧ Tool #17 – Emotion Coaching
"I can tell you are really struggling with this." And after listening actively, do a Problem Solving session (see below).

Solutions requiring a little more time or practice

❧ Tool #20 – Growth Mindset
To foster your child's self-esteem and confidence, use the 10 steps to developing a Growth Mindset.

❧ Tool #21 – Problem-Solving (age 3+)
"What could *you* do to make this easier for you? Do you want to know what other children have tried?"

17. Wanting your constant attention

Children naturally crave their parents' attention, and it is only natural that we should want to give them as much of our attention as possible. However, this can prove to be difficult when we are stretched for time and overloaded with work and their demands for our attention are constant. It's actually important to give the 'right' attention to children to make sure we don't create a self-reinforcing cycle of wanting more attention. So rather than losing our patience or temper and stressing ourselves out even further, we can save ourselves much time and energy by choosing to implement one of the following tools instead:

Quick and easy solutions: 5 minutes max

᠙ Tool #6 – Limited Choices
Ensure that your child does as many things as possible on his/her own so that they feel more empowered, and to allow you to use as many Limited Choices as possible.

᠙ Tool #7 – Asking Questions
"Do you think I can give you my full attention if you keep interrupting me while I am finishing something that is important to me?"

᠙ Tool #8 – Positive & Enforceable Statements
"I help children who have already tried to do things by themselves."

᠙ Tool #15 – Family Contribution
Involve your child in as many household tasks as possible. This is one of the keys to reducing the attention-seeking as it makes our children feel more important.

Solutions requiring a little more time or practice

᠙ Tool #5 – Creating Routines
Devise a routine (ideally with your child's help) and then stick to it, allowing this routine rather than you, to become the boss.

᠙ Tool #16 – Presence (Aka One-on-one Time)
Dedicate some regular one-to-one 'quality' time between yourself and your child. It is a great way to encourage your child to feel more significant.

ᔋ Tool #21 – Problem-Solving (age 3+)
"When you constantly ask me for my attention I can't complete any of my tasks, what could we do to make you feel that we have enough time together?". And obviously quitting your job is not on the list of options!

18. Lying or Fabricating

Lying and fabricating, whilst being a perfectly natural part of a child's development, can be difficult for parents to deal with. It's hurtful and unpleasant when we know that our child is lying to us or fabricating stories to other people. However, lying often stems from our reactions to our children's misdeeds. Rather than blaming ourselves and allowing it to damage the connection we have with our child, we can deal with it by following these step-by-step and easy-to-apply tools:

Quick and easy solutions: 5 minutes max

ᔋ Tool #7 – Asking Questions
"Do you think that I'll be able to trust you in the future if you lie to me about certain things?"

ᔋ Tool #11 – Setting Rules/Clarifying Expectations
"In this family we value truth telling above all else."

Solutions requiring a little more time or practice

ᔋ Tool #19 – Logical & Delayed Consequences
"Unfortunately since you have lied about having done your homework, we're going to have to stay in this weekend to make sure that you do it."
Or delayed: "Sadly, because you lied to me yesterday and claimed that you hadn't taken your sister's sweets, I won't be buying you a treat today."
Or: "When I hear lies it gives me an energy drain, I'll need your help getting some energy back!"

ᔋ Tool #21 – Problem-Solving (age 3+)

This is the most important tool for solving 'communication' issues, such as lying, because it ensures that you have a proper conversation with your child about why it is so important to tell the truth

For example, "I feel disappointed when you lie to me, because it makes it very difficult for me and others to trust you. Since telling the truth is really important, what do you think might discourage you from telling lies in the future?"

19. Disrespecting House Rules

When our children refuse to follow or disrespect our household rules, it makes it difficult to enjoy the time that we get to spend with them because we are constantly having to nag and remind them to do things in the way we would expect. This issue can become even more problematic when the time we get to spend with our children is limited in the first place. If we're at work all day, we may be too tired to enforce our rules, or we simply don't want to enter into a conflict with our child, so we end up 'letting things slide' and family harmony becomes ever more elusive as a result. To prevent your child from disrespecting the household rules that you have set in a way that doesn't damage the connection you have with them, try using one of the following tools:

Quick and easy solutions: 5 minutes max

⤷ Tool #7 – Asking Questions
"How we do things in this house?"

⤷ Tool #8 – Positive & Enforceable Statements
"I do things for children who respect our family rules."

⤷ Tool #11 – Setting Rules/Clarifying Expectations
It is helpful to ask your child to make a list of the house rules that they can remember (in a caring kind of way) and then ask them to explain back to you why they think the rules are there.

Solutions requiring a little more time or practice

ᕱ Tool #19 – Logical & Delayed Consequences
"What a shame, as you know our rule is that we remain seated for our meals, and since you left the table to go play, dinner is now over for you."
Or delayed: "Sadly, since you broke the rule about fighting in the car, I'm now not going to be able to take you on that trip to the ice cream parlour."

ᕱ Tool #21 – Problem-Solving (age 3+)
"You seem to have difficulty following the house rules, what do you suggest we do to make sure that you don't break them again in the future?"

20. Hassling-Pestering Behaviour

When our mind is on other things and our child is hassling or pestering us for attention, we can often find ourselves getting triggered and either giving in to their 'mis'behaviour or losing our temper with them and shouting at them for it. Trying to send an important work email while our child is pulling at our sleeve is something that almost every working parent can relate to! Next time you find yourself in this situation, you can regain control and prevent it from escalating by implementing the following step-by-step tools:

Quick and easy solutions: 5 minutes max

ᕱ Tool #7 – Asking Questions
"Do you think that nagging will make it more likely that I do what you ask of me?"

ᕱ Tool #9 – Positive Redirection
"Yes, you can have this chocolate bar, but you'll have to wait for snack time."

✎ Tool #17 – Emotion Coaching

"I can see that you really, really want me to take you to the soft play centre, but unfortunately, it's not going to be possible now." And then repeat an 'empathetic statement' like "I know", or "I heard you", or "I love you too much to argue" until they stop nagging.

Solutions requiring a little more time or practice

✎ Tool #19 – Logical & Delayed Consequences

"Your insistence is causing me an energy drain, I'll need your help getting some energy back if you'd like me to take you where you want to go later."

✎ Tool #21 – Problem-Solving (age 3+)

"You have been constantly asking for things today and it has become pretty annoying. What do you think would be a better way of getting my attention?"

Endnotes

[1] Friedman, Steward - *Leading the Life You Want: Skills for Integrating Work and Life*, Harvard Business Review Press, 2014

[2] K. Kruse, Kevin, http://www.forbes.com/sites/kevinkruse/2013/04/09/what-is-leadership, 2013

[3] Gordon, Thomas, *Parent Effectiveness Training*, Three River Press, 2000

[4] Johnson, Sara, Blum, Robert, Giedd, Jay, *Adolescent Maturity and the Brain: The Promise and Pitfalls of Neuroscience Research in Adolescent Health Policy*, Journal of Adolescent Health, Sep 2009

[5] Bronson, Po and Merryman, Ashley, *Nurture Shock*, Ebury Press, 2009

[6] Baumrind, Diana, *Effects of Authoritative Parental Control on Child Behavior*, Child Development, 1966

[7] Baumrind, Diana, *Childcare practices anteceding three patterns of preschool behaviour*, Genetic Psychology Monographs, 1967

[8] Baumrind, Diana, *Childcare practices anteceding three patterns of preschool behavior*

[9] Baumrind, Diana *Effects of Authoritative Parental Control on Child Behavior*

[10] William Glasser, *Theory of Choice*, Harper Perennial, 2007

[11] Sara B. Johnson, Ph.D., M.P.H,[a,*] Robert W. Blum, M.D., Ph.D,[b] and Jay N. Giedd, M.D[c]

Adolescent Maturity and the Brain: The Promise and Pitfalls of Neuroscience Research in Adolescent Health Policy

[12] Molly Edmonds, Are teenage brains really different from adult brains?, American Psychological Association, 2008

[13] Judith E Glaser, Conversational intelligence, Bibliomotion, 2013

[14] Lea Winerman, *The mind's mirror*, American Psychological Association, 2005

[15] Steve Peters, *The Chimp paradox.*, Vermilion, 2012

[16] Sunderland, Margot, *What every parent needs to know*, Dorling Kindersley, 2007

[17] Siegel, Daniel, *Parenting From the Inside Out*, Jeremy P. Tarcher, 2003

[18] Warneken and Tomasello, *Extrinsic rewards undermine altruistic tendencies in 20-month-olds*, 2006/7

[19] David, Susan, *Emotional Agility*, Penguin Life, 2016

[20] Webster-Stratton, *The Incredible Years*, Incredible Years, 2005

[21] Ginott, Haim, *Between Parent and Child*, Crown Publications, 2004

[22] McGinn, Kathleen L., Mayra Ruiz Castro, and Elizabeth Long Lingo, *Mums the Word! Cross-national Relationship between Maternal Employment and Gender Inequalities at Work and at Home*, June 2015.

[23] David, Susan, *Emotional Agility*, Penguin Life, 2016

24 Covey, Steven, *7 principles of highly effective families*, Simon & Schuster UK; New Ed edition, 1999

25 Cohen, Lawrence, *Playful Parenting*, Ballantine Books, 2012

26 Siegel, Daniel, *The Whole Brain Child*, Bantam, 2012

27 Neufeld, Gordon, *Hold on to your kids*, Ballantine Books, 2006

28 Karson, Michael, Psychology Today, https://www.psychologytoday.com/blog/feeling-our-way/201401/punishment-doesnt-work, 2014

29 Kohn, Alfie, http://www.alfiekohn.org/parenting/punishment.htm, 2005

30 Nelsen, Jane, *Positive Discipline*, Ballantine Books, 2013

31 Dweck, Carol, *Mindset: The New Psychology of Success*, Ballantine Books, 2007

32 Siegel, Daniel, *Parenting From the Inside Out*, Jeremy P. Tarcher, 2003

Resources and Further Reading

Aldort, Naomi, *Raising our Children, Raising Ourselves*, Book Publishers Network, 2005

Bronson, Po and Merryman, Ashley, *Nurture Shock*, Ebury Press, 2009

Biddulph, Steve, Raising Boys, Harper Thorsons, 2010

Biddulph, Steve, Raising Girls, Harper, 2013

Carey, Tanith, *Mum Hacks - Time-saving tips to calm the chaos of family life*, White Ladder Press, 2016

Carey, Tanith, *Taming the Tiger Parent*, Robinson, 2014

Carey, Tanith, *Girls Uninterrupted: Steps for Building Stronger Girls in a Challenging World*, Icon Books, 2015

Cohen, Lawrence, Playful Parenting, Ballantine Books, 2012

David, Susan, *Emotional Agility*, Penguin Life, 2016

Dreikurs, Rudolf, *Children: The Challenge*, First Plume Printing, 1990

Dweck, Carol, *Mindset: The New Psychology of Success*, Ballantine Books, 2007

Faber, Adele and Mazlish, Elaine, *How to Talk so Kids Will Listen and Listen so Kids Will Talk*, Avon Books, 1999

Faber, Adele and Mazlish, Elaine, *Siblings Without Rivalry*, Piccadilly Press, 1999

Fay, Jim and Cline, Foster, *Parenting with Love and Logic*, Navpress, 2006

Fay, Jim and Charles, *Love and Logic Magic for Early Childhood*, Love and Logic, 2000

Gordon, Thomas, *Parent Effectiveness Training*, Three River Press, 2000

Goleman, Daniel, *Emotional Intelligence: Why it Can Matter More Than IQ*, Bloomsbury, 1996

Gottman, John, *Raising an Emotionally Intelligent Child*, Simon and Chuster, 1997

Ginott, Haim, *Between Parent and Child*, Crown Publications, 2004

Hawn, Goldie, *10 Mindful minutes*, Piatkus, 2011

Ibarra, Herminia, *Act Like a Leader, Think Like a Leader*, Harvard Business Review Press, 2015

James, Oliver, *They F*** You Up: How to Survive Family Life*, Bloomsbury, 2006

James, Oliver, *How not to f*** them up*, Vermillion, 2011

Kohn, Alfie, *Unconditional Parenting*, Atria Books, 2005

Kohn, Alfie, *Punished by Rewards*, Houghton Mifflin, 2000

Lenzer Kirk, Julie, *The parentpreneur edge*, John Wiley & Sons, 2007

Markham, Laura, *Peaceful Parent, Happy Kids*, Penguin Books, 2012

Medina, John, *Brain Rules - 12 principles for surviving and thriving at work, home and school*, Pear Press, 2014

Mischel, Walter, *The Marshmallow Test: Mastering Self-control*, Little Brown and Company, 2014

Nelsen, Jane, *Positive Discipline*, Ballantine Books, 2013

Nelsen, Jane and Lott, Lynn, and Glen, Stephen, *A-Z*, Three Rivers Press, 2007

Mc Cready, Amy, *If I Have To Tell You One More Time*, Penguin, 2012

Palmer, Sue, *Toxic Childhood*, Orion Books, 2007

Palmer, Sue, *Detoxing Childhood*, Orion Books, 2008

Reivich, Karen and Shatte, Andrew, *The Resilience Factor*, Three Rivers Press, 2002

Sanders, Matthew, *Every Parent*, Penguin Books, 2004

Shefali Tsabary, *The Conscious Parent: Transforming Ourselves, Empowering Our Children*, Namaste Publishing, 2010

Siegel, Daniel, Hartzell, Mary, *Parenting From the Inside Out*, Jeremy P. Tarcher, 2003

Siegel, Daniel, Bryson Payne, Tine, *The Whole Brain Child*, Bantam, 2012

Stoll Lillard, Angeline, *Montessori - The science behind the genius*, Oxford University Press, 2007

Sunderland, Margot, *What every parent needs to know*, Dorling Kindersley, 2007

Webster-Stratton, *The Incredible Years*, Incredible Years, 2005

Acknowledgements

I would like to give credit to all the inspiring people who've dedicated their lives to improving parenting and child development all over the world, and without whom creating our content and tools would not have been possible, such as: Jane Nelsen of Positive Discipline, Jim and Charles Fay of Love and Logic, Alfie Kohn, Daniel Siegel, John Gottman, Laura Markham, Haim Ginott, Adele Faber and Elaine Mazlish, Rudolf Dreikurs, Alfred Adler, Maria Montessori and many more!

I would like to thank my Copywriter, Hollie Sherrington, whose contribution and dedication has been invaluable in writing this book.

I also want to thank my Editor, Jacq Burns, for her support over the years and for her expert advice.

Thank you also to Denise Dampierre with who I co-wrote the tool Family Values and whose input has been valuable.

Last but not least, thank you to all the experts and friends who have spent time reading the drafts of my manuscript to give me very useful feedback. Just to name a few: Tanith Carey, John Lees, Garry Leboff, Andrew Coppin, Mark and Zaz Peatey, Michael Kouly, Jerôme Ballarin, Caroline Vanovermeire, Kirstie Sneyd, Louise Walewska, Teresa Marinetti, Almudena Sevilla, Jessica and Roland Stapper, Cor Dubois, Anoma Baste, Michael Hirt, Liza Lovdahl, Lata Gullapalli and Liz Lian.

Index